Reflections on
Unconditional Communication

I wrote this book convinced that communication is not one thing, it's the only thing we have to connect and co-create the world we want to live in. I am grateful for the reflections I have received from friends and clients around the world, who have reviewed advance copies of this book and seen the relevance of *Unconditional Communication* to different contexts and applications. Thank you, all.

David

I have worked for Mars for nearly 20 years. It is a values-based company and stays true to its Five Principles. David's extraordinary approach to communication and leadership has helped me, and many of my colleagues, authentically lead from the ground we stand on. It has helped me be better not only at work leading a factory or leadership teams, but also at home and in the community. This book can help you be an excellent communicator, but most of all an authentic leader who understands their values and uses them as a crucial strength!

Jeroen van Vlerken, Mars Supply Excellence Lead - Europe

David and I met when he was coaching me during my transition from General Manager at PayPal Latam to become what I did not know then: a Civic Entrepreneur. Communication is the strongest human behavior for interaction within our society. The book brings some very strong messages, including: 'your speaking awakens an already-there seed.' For me, I was challenged to realize that 'the formless that I want to make into form' is HOPE. Leaders must act to bring hope - and 'communication as an act of service' (another of David's messages) is critical to that shared story.

Mario Mello, Founder & CEO "Poder do Voto" app - Brazil

I have read all of David's books since he first published The Corporate Fool in 1998 and have enjoyed every one. Always out on the edge of management thinking about what it takes to succeed in complex organizations, he has turned his decades of experience in helping business leaders be more impactful to people and society at large. Imagine a world of bigger, better relationships and futures for all. A world where everyone's voice is heard, where there is trust and connection and where we create futures together...this is the promise of "unconditional communication". This is perhaps a new manifesto for individuals, families, societies and political systems to thrive in a post Covid-19 world.

Peter Attfield
Chief Talent & Learning Officer
Jardine Matheson, Hong Kong

Never has communication been more important - and never have we seen more clearly the devastating effects of a world based on shouting and judging. Effective communication requires conscious speaking and conscious listening, two skills that fashion our outcomes in life and that anchor both civil society and family relationships - but that are not taught in school. This book is about the why of communication, as David makes an incontrovertible case for what he calls unconditional communication - in essence, a process of giving rather than grasping. We need this book!

Julian Treasure, author of *How To Be Heard*
and five-time TED speaker

I sincerely wish I could have internalized the wisdom I find in your words when I was on the front end of my professional career. At the same time, I believe your words are best internalized by those who sense they need to take their leadership to another level and have the courage to be honest with themselves. It truly touches the soul. This is a must read for anyone in a leadership position.

Dr Stan Scheer, Four-Time School Superintendent

We all agree that great things are never built on small relationships - this book outlines in a great way that small relationships are a consequence of what and how we communicate. The 'where we come from' when we communicate is a great insight that will shift the paradigm from 'communicate to persuade' to 'communicate to do good.' For all of us who would like to make a positive impact in the world this is crucial reading!

AJ van Triest - CEO Fitchannel.com -
Client and Friend of David.

A joyful rebel fueled by curiosity, humility, and a well-spring of wisdom, David Firth lays bare the illusion of separateness between us humans and lights the path toward connectedness, acceptance, and love in interaction. Let this book equip you for the future!

Bennett Bratt, CEO and Founder of
The Team Effectiveness Project and author
of The Team Discovered: Dialogic Team Coaching

David has written such a beautiful book. If ever you've been in unconditional communication you'll know what he's talking about and you'll want to be there whenever possible. If not, then read this. Actually, either way you should read this. It may be about letting go, though it may be more about letting be. Plus it features a story about a skip near Newcastle that can never be bettered.

Neil Mullarkey, Founder of London's Comedy Store Players and author of *Seven Steps to Improve Your People Skills*

This book helped me remember that my intention has been always to put my best to serving others, but sometimes I forgot why. Unconditional Communication is the elbow on the ribs needed to remember that we can be of value to others without having to learn something new, but by untapping the love that is already inside us, and open up to co-create the world we want.

Maye Alessandrini, CHRO Softys - A CMPC Company

Scientists (truth seekers) and engineers (problem solvers) should heed David's advice in "Unconditional Communication" to set aside their and their tribe's a priori favorites and engage in truly open - 'formless' as David writes - dialog to better create shared knowledge and solutions.

Kevin Lear, Professor, Colorado State University.

Highly resonant today! Understanding the meaning of "Unconditional Communication" is the key to our collective future, which is more important now than ever before. This book helps us realize that we have the power to change the world through communication, and why we must do it *together*.

Melinda May, Former Vice President Marketing
Strategy at the International Olympic Committee

You may be surprised to see words like creation, loneliness, hero and love in a book about communication. But if you know David Firth then you know how powerfully he can frame the topic in a way that can simply transform the way you approach communication. And, in fact, life in general.

Ricardo Pimenta, General Manager and
Vice-President, Pepsico

UNCONDITIONAL COMMUNICATION

Shaping Better Relationships and Bigger Futures - Together

David Firth

All on a journey, and not done yet...

ISBN: 978-0-9854945-1-3

Copyright © 2020 David Firth.

Lagado Library Publications, Colorado, USA

Printed in the United States of America.

First printing, 2020.

www.davidfirth.com

Cover Design: Johnnie Stephens

Copyediting: Trey Davis

Interior Design: Andrea Reider

Contents

The focus of this book in creating a world we
want to live in:

1. Bigger Futures

2. Better Relationships

3. Together

The three foundations of Unconditional Communication:

1. Presence
   - Incredibly fun, but rare
2. Connection
   - Communication as an act of service
3. Created Outcomes
   - Speak like your words matter

Little Victories or Bigger Callings?

- Your role in the upward spiral

- Really, Town Halls are not such a great idea

- Where's next for us?

Dedication

My Dad, Alan Worrall Firth, showed me Unconditional Communication, mostly from what he didn't do rather than what he did. Never a wasted word. Zero desire to involve himself in gossip. Rarely a passionate complaint. If he did have a beef with someone or something, he'd deliver it in a soft and understated way. He didn't like Woody Allen's comedy, for some reason (and I remind you this was long before the revelations about Allen's complex love life) but even if there'd been Twitter back then, he just would not have felt the need to share his opinion about Woody Allen's comedy that widely. He wasn't desperate to be heard, which made him a compelling communicator when he spoke.

He also showed me - in his own beautiful, quiet and grounded way - what a spiritual life could be like on this earth. He was a lay preacher in the Church of England - basically the highest stage you can get to in the Church without actually going the whole hog and becoming an ordained priest. So he devoted a lot of his life to his faith and the church community. At his funeral, I saw how much he was revered for that work.

In addition to that, he worked most of his career at a locally-based haulage company. Many Sundays, after church, he would take me there so he could inspect the drivers' cabs as part of his job. I saw my first naked women on those visits, because that was the age of nude calendars and softcore mags, both of which were readily apparent in that workplace. And I heard my first curse words there too.

And my Dad was the same man in both those environments, sacred church and profane workplace. He didn't change because of who or what was in front of him. He didn't judge or dismiss. His communication was always about what he felt was best for others, in their situation. Or it was silence.

There is something else from this little life history. There were times, as a youngster, I felt I was being dragged to church. Not always, but sometimes. There was one moment of great significance to me, as a boy, when I missed a BBC2 TV documentary about poisonous spiders because my Dad's sermon during Evensong went on too long, IMHO. But I am over that now. And what all those years of going to church left me with was not a continued trust in organized religion - it certainly did not do that - but an enduring sense that life has depth, and that there might be more to it than what is going on at the surface level. Had he just taken me to see Leeds United every other Saturday, I might have been left with the understanding that life is 6 days of obligation - school in my case, work in his - relieved by one day of exhilaration and pleasure at a sports event. Instead Dad taught me that life has meaning, and purpose, and is precious.

And I am beyond grateful for everything my Dad, Alan Worrall Firth, taught me.

Acknowledgements

The book you are about to read is unashamedly a testament to the power of Love and the potential of the human species. Nowhere in my life is that more present than in the form of my wife, Keri. I know you want to get another dog, babe, but no other being on the planet will try to show you more unconditional love and gratitude than I try my ridiculous best to show you every day. Thank you for bursting into my life, 35 years ago.

I find myself talking regularly about my three sons, Oliver, Sam and Alex, in my workshops and my books. On one level, this is a technique: I am trying to demonstrate that I am another dude with kids, just like you. The reality is I am in awe of the fact that I get to be around who they are being in the world.

I have dedicated this book to my Dad, whose influence on me you will read on just about every page. It doesn't surprise me either, given the nature of The Hero's Journey, that I am writing this final page of the book when my Mum is with us in Colorado, visiting from her home in West Yorkshire,

England. Thank you, Mum. These are special times, among a life of wonder. And I am so thrilled we got to watch *The War of the Worlds* together.

Alan Leigh founded The Lords of Misrule with me after our time at Oxford. He went on to have a hugely successful career in banking, and whatever impact he might have had on people around the globe in that work, I know he exploded me out of a box I had built for myself when we first met, which I'd labelled 'Limited Potential.' Thank you, my friend.

Trey Davis has been an extraordinarily perceptive and sensitive editor of this book. And also the owner of the best Skype profile icon I've seen.

It's all an upward spiral, and the relationship I have had with my tutors, back in my literature days, and then my audiences, in my theater days, and more recently with all my clients in the last 30 years, has been a testament to that. Whatever I might have given to others, I received from others before, and it all spins, always and in all ways, upward and outward.

IT IS I WHO MUST BEGIN

It is I who must begin.
Once I begin, once I try —
here and now,
right where I am,
not excusing myself
by saying things
would be easier elsewhere,
without grand speeches and
ostentatious gestures,
but all the more persistently
— to live in harmony
with the "voice of Being," as I
understand it within myself
— as soon as I begin that,
I suddenly discover,
to my surprise, that
I am neither the only one,
nor the first,
nor the most important one
to have set out
upon that road.
Whether all is really lost
or not depends entirely on
whether or not I am lost.

~ Václav Havel ~

IT IS I WHO MUST BEGIN

It is I who must begin.
Once I begin, once I try —
here and now,
right where I am,
not excusing myself
by saying things
would be easier elsewhere,
without grand speeches and
ostentatious gestures,
but all the more persistently
— to live in harmony
with the "voice of Being," as I
understand it within myself
— as soon as I begin that,
I suddenly discover,
to my surprise, that
I am neither the only one,
nor the first,
nor the most important one
to have set out
upon that road.
Whether all is really lost
or not depends entirely on
whether or not I am lost.

~ Václav Havel ~

INTRODUCTION

THIS IS NOT THE BOOK YOU WERE LOOKING FOR. (PROBABLY).

The book you were probably looking for is the *How To* book. I'm working on that now and it is called *How to Communicate Good* and it will be available soon.

But that book is not this one.

We live in a world where *How do we?* or *How do I?* seem to be the only questions we ask any more. Our society worships practicality, application, execution and instant results - as if more of what we've been addicted to for many years will get us out of the situation we are in.

These questions of practicality are valid for simple problems - and we have created channels for finding answers for most of them. Last week, our refrigerator stopped dispensing ice, but a short conference with Auntie YouTube and Uncle Google helped me sort it out.

But to ask for easy answers to complex challenges – of which human communication is a perfect example – is an avoidance of responsibility. To demand tips and techniques when we know that we are faced with complexity and paradox, is to avoid our role in shaping something better. We ought to be able to step back and think; human beings have been communicating since the earliest forms of human life, and using language for around 100,000 years of that time. That we've been trying it out so much and still failing so badly to connect and collaborate, is worthy of consideration. If practice makes perfect, ours must be a steep learning curve. It seems that being human together is not, and will never be, like dispensing ice from my fridge.

And in many ways, if you think about it, haven't we mastered the 'How to...' of communication already? Exactly how far across the planet do you need your friend to move before they can't text you in an instant? You can reach just about anyone, anywhere. That's powerful.

And we have access to more information than we have the life left to process it. There's no shortage of 'what' to do. If you need to mend your fridge, help is at hand. If you type 'How to communicate' into Google, you get 308,000,000 results in 0.92 seconds. And yet here we are. All the connectivity we could ever use, but little sense of real connection.

Quite the contrary, in fact. We know exactly *How to* communicate in order to disconnect from each other. We know how to belittle, shame, provoke, demean and undermine each other.

No-one is writing books on those skills, because we seem to have mastered them. Some people can communicate so well on the internet that they can cause others to commit suicide. Four hundred years ago they'd have called that ability magic, or demonic.

And that is why my own *How to* book is not called *How to Communicate At All* but *How to Communicate Good.*

But that book is not this one. In this book, I invite you to spend some time doing some currently unsexy things, such as stepping back, slowing down and reflecting.

What does it require for us to use communication as an expression of the best in us, rather than a vehicle for the worst of us?

And how can you consider less the *How* and the *What* you are communicating - but *Where you are coming from* when you communicate?

Communication is how we make the world we live in. I believe that's worth some consideration - or at least the 200 pages of a book.

AND THIS IS PROBABLY NOT THE WORLD YOU HAD IN MIND

Does it seem to you that the world right now seems back to front and upside down? Does the world seem to you more fraught, anxious and fractured than it was only some years back?

Communication is not only how we create, but also how we experience this discombobulation. We see, hear, and feel the noise, the fury, the harshness of speaking, the threats and jibes. The tone of despair on one side – or the tone of barely moderated glee, on the other – when some public figure has slipped up, or done or said something that might bring them down.

We all seem to be always on the edge of wanting someone to win, and someone to lose.

How long has it been since our public discourse was characterized by curiosity or compassion or forgiveness? Maybe it never was. But I would suggest that there is a level of mutual aggression and bitterness that has now overtaken public dialogue, and with it a devil-may-care attitude to the impact of our words.

> *The notion of a threatened democracy has been fueled by hyper-partisanship, political gridlock, divisive rhetoric, conspiracy theories spread by social media and concerns of voter fraud. But, the true threat to civil discourse is the rejection of the need for civility in representing the will of the people. President Donald Trump's reference to African countries and Haiti as "shit hole countries" is a poignant example of the use of language... [and the] impacts and implications of the use of this language are felt beyond the confines of his utterance.*

Vanessa Lopez-Littleton

This aggression now reverberates around the echo chambers of social media, leaping out of the political domain and across categories such as business, music, entertainment, celebrity life and sport. On the BBC Sport app, 'Your post is awaiting moderation' is often seen in the discussion threads, when someone has had a racist, or otherwise offensive, comment deleted. Truly, if ever you need to deflate any optimism you hold for the human race, simply spend some time browsing the discussion threads of any news outlet, and see how quickly any sensible debate can hurtle downwards into name-calling and spiteful disregard of others. If anger ultimately is always rooted in fear, then a lot of us must be very afraid.

Maybe that's because we've become immersed in – and created for ourselves – a world where someone else might win, and there's only so much winning to go around. The competitive urge in human nature has never been so nourished as it is now. In my youth, Fanny Cradock (Google her), and later Keith Floyd, used to step gingerly around their TV studio kitchens and show us how to make something we might like to eat. Their passion for food, and their ability to inspire us to replicate their efforts, *was* the entertainment. Now, many cookery shows have become competitions where the drama of losing and being cast out is the main reason to watch. So too, the same is true of programs about singing, dancing, and even entrepreneurship (life's a Shark Tank, folks). In the days of the Roman Empire, it was the Emperor who decided life or death. Now it is 'the panel of experts.'

And when most of us spend, on average, 6 hours and 43 minutes per waking day locked into a screen of some kind, all this hectic, win/lose energy can only seep through into the everyday life of individuals, of you and me. Any personal anxiety can only be heightened by watching so many examples of the apparently thin line between triumph and humiliation. And by the constant reminder that someone else will be the one to determine that outcome.

We are left then with a zeitgeist, a cultural climate that vacillates between aggression and despair.

Once a society loses this capacity [for dialogue], all that's left is a cacophony of voices battling it out to see who wins and who loses. There is no capacity to go deeper, to find a deeper meaning that transcends individual views and self-interest. It seems reasonable to ask whether many of our deeper problems in governing ourselves, the so-called gridlock and loss of mutual respect and caring might not stem from this lost capacity to talk with one another and to think together as part of the larger community.

Peter Senge

And here's the thing. Here's why I am offering you this book.

What I would characterize as an emerging loss of hope and optimism at a societal level is a threat to the soul at an individual level.

What does the soul seek? What are we all seeking, beneath differences of personality type, creed, color or politics?

Presence, I would suggest. A sense of being fully, and happily, alive.

And a feeling of true connection - to each other, and to a shared purpose.

And a particular identity of worthiness and agency: a sense that we matter and can make a difference. That we can be the change we seek in the world.

Presence, Connection and Agency. Unconditional Communication can bring those things about.

The old paradigm - what I call conditional communication - is broken. The old paradigm is not concerned with Presence, Connection, and Agency, but is focused most on the art of persuasion: one person persuading others. Our job has been reduced to choosing who we are most going to be persuaded by. And that can veer too often into a form of creepy manipulation.

The old paradigm is based on presentation and surface - it's about looking good and sounding strong. Communication is not seen as something that could bring us together. It is reduced to the consideration of how other people impact us.

Go to any conference or event, and the feedback forms will focus on two areas: does the speaker have good content, and do they present it well? Beneath those apparently sensible feedback questions is the idea that the communication is happening 'over there' i.e. where the speaker is - and our role is to grade that performance. We get to be one of the 'panel of experts' deciding what's good and what's bad. What happens as a result of the speaker's speaking is not asked about in the feedback. What grows or comes from it is not measured. What changes in our world, because of what is said, is not captured or, apparently, valued. And our role in creating that possible future is not considered.

All that matters is that we have had an experience. The conference people want to make sure it was a good experience, or we might not come back next year, but the outcome is otherwise unimportant, even incidental. This old paradigm emphasis on the speaker's 'impactful skills' - that we are a result of someone else's speaking - has encouraged us to ask for more satisfaction. Now we want communication that is faster and easy to consume. I was at a dinner with friends last night where everyone agreed that it feels nice to be inspired and educated by any speaker, but is there any chance we could get that result quicker? We're all so very busy, after all. It was agreed a video of someone speaking should be about a minute in length. 'If I see it's going to take any longer than that, I'll go to the transcript and take what I want from there,' said one.

One minute.

And this idea that we are consuming - and not co-creating - communication has led us into the current world of the snappy soundbite, the easily told anecdote, the retweet, the quippy Facebook comment. And despite the fact that many of us complain about how shallow social discourse is becoming, all of that will continue as long as we agree to play the part of 'being too busy to think.' I don't care what you think of Trump and his politics, but critical thinking is not what he is selling, or seeking. We're not going to change that reality by asking for better tweets.

Speaking at a conference, I once got 12 out of 10 on a feed-back form[1]. The person was so - at the moment of them filling out the feedback form - moved and inspired by my presentation that they added some dotted lines after the 10 maximum, wrote the number 12, and circled that. When the conference people shared that with me, my ego was delighted. But did anything of lasting value actually come from that, for that person or others? And how would I know? Because the old paradigm of communication doesn't care to seek that answer.

And besides, the emphasis on communication being about 'strong speaking skills' only results in giving us more of what

---

1. I am sure there are many times people have wanted to give me -2 out of 10, but my argument stands.

we don't need. Because the skills themselves are powerful, but in themselves might distract from our greater good.

When we begin to think about all the noise thrown at us by politicians, the news media, corporations in their advertising, we can begin to see something worrying. The very things we have revered in 'good communication' - confidence, clarity, courage and a level of charisma - we now see to be the same tools that can bring us down, as much as raise us up, depending on who has the microphone. Hitler was a terrific story-teller. He was not a barrel of laughs, apparently, but Lord, he got shit done. Why should that devil have all the best tunes?

Now, I agree that we should teach those skills in a way that spreads the mastery of communication from the few to the many. The Hitlers of the world will always discover the secrets of storytelling, because they know that it can captivate the masses - so I want to make those same skills available to all the non-Hitlers too. I would like every school age child to own the wonderful experience of knowing what they want to say, and being able to say it with energy and enthusiasm. For every individual using those same skills to communicate evil, I want two people using them to communicate good.

And we don't have to be on TED.com to practice that. Not many of us will ever want, or need, to get on a stage and give a keynote speech with our 'strong platform skills' - but which of us would not value more intentionality in our daily communication with loved ones and colleagues? Or more clarity in what we want to say, or the hope that it might impact others constructively? Which of us would not benefit in being more able to ask for what we want? Or to communicate what we don't want by asserting our boundaries and needs in relationships with others? Which of us would not want to know how to help, or how to most effectively offer that help?

In this book, then, I am going to look at what it takes to be confident and courageous in your speaking, to be more clear in your articulation, to manage conflict - whenever you are communicating, to whomever, about whatever really matters to you.

But skills are only on the surface level. Anyone can learn them.

The real difference is where you are coming from when you use those skills. That is the new paradigm I argue for in this book. A new paradigm for communication that encourages a transition *from self to service.*

I want to encourage you to talk as a service to others, rather than communication being something you do to get something from others.

And the aim of this book is not to argue for this paradigm shift and then to have you wait to see if it happens in the public discourse. It won't. Not yet, if ever. Our political and institutional constructions are built on the foundation of the few leading the many. Our organizations and institutions encourage and reward those strong 'selves' who appear to be there to serve us, but in fact have something in mind for us. Many of them are genuinely well-intentioned, but deep down they are trying to sell us something. You and I might want to reflect on our impulse to buy what they are selling.

No leader came to power in the modern world by selling alone; they depended on our complicity in buying it. And that creates a predictable outcome. I would argue that the history of civilisation is the history of a dual dynamic:

1. A brief period of excitement with a new leader (a new boss, a new pastor, a new Board of Education, a new President),

and then:

2. A shift into profound disappointment with those very leaders, whether that dismay happens suddenly or eventually.

We might want to look at our part in that dynamic of wanting to keep buying the same goods only to be disappointed - no matter how the presentation of those goods might make us feel. We have to step up from being consumers.

The epitome of what I call outside-in thinking is that someone is coming to save us - we just need to listen for the next best one. But no-one is coming.

Most of all, I want to suggest in this book that being a good consumer of others' stuff - whatever it is, including mine - is not the highest expression of your life. And that the alternative is to be a creator of what you are looking for.

In the old Bible story, God *spoke* the world into being. And so can you, with your world.

WE ARE EXACTLY WHAT WE HAVE BEEN SEEKING

I'm 8 years old and I am standing on the chancel steps of All Saints Church, Churwell, in England.

My Dad, the lay reader, is getting everything ready for the next Sunday service. He beckons me forward toward the altar, where he is arranging the candles and prayer books and communion plate, and turning the Bible open to the requisite page for the first lesson of the next service.

Being invited to move from the chancel steps to stand before the altar is, for me, crossing a threshold of great magnitude. This is a place usually occupied only by the priest, the servers and the choir. I feel in awe of taking those few simple steps forward to join my Dad.

I gaze at this familiar scene from a different place, in all senses of that phrase.

Behind the altar are two tall, blue pillars, each with a golden angel at the top. The pillars hold between them a giant, red velvet curtain.

I ask my Dad: 'Dad, what's behind the curtain?'

Even at that young age, I know that, technically, there is a wall behind the curtain, and, behind that, the church's parking lot.

But, even at that young age, I am somehow aware that there are different levels of reality.

'Dad, what's behind the curtain?' I ask again.

Dad stops what he is doing, looks at me, and says, gently: 'God is behind the curtain.'

At 8 years old, if you'd asked me to draw God, I'd have drawn you a kind old man with a white beard, floating on clouds. But I sensed, already, that there was more to it than that.

So I asked my Dad: 'What does God look like?'

My Dad was not one of those Christians whose default reaction was to answer any difficult questions by quoting scripture, but he did say:

'God made Man in His own image, David.'

So God is not an old man with a beard. And surely God does not look like me, David. So what on earth does 'in His own image mean?'

48 years later, I now know what that scripture means. It means two things:

God made human beings out of the Formless, and into Form.

We Are Exactly What We Have Been Seeking

And

God made human beings in his own likeness, which is, the likeness of a loving Creator.

God created. And human beings get to create too.

You can drop the religious aspect of this section if you are more comfortable. You can erase any mention of God.

But I am of the profound conviction that humankind is a creator.

After 30 years of consulting and coaching, I have never come across a situation, problem, or barrier my clients face that was not created by Humankind.

And therefore any change for the better will be created by Humankind too.

If this book is a manifesto, then it is truly a grassroots one. It is almost a cliché now to use the phrase 'It starts with you.' But this change does - or it won't become change at all.

Your communication is a creative act. And it is spoken. In the Bible story of Genesis, God did not wish the Heavens and the Earth into being. He did not hope that there was Light. He did not draw a Vision Board, He *said* so.

And that's how you will create your future too. By *speaking* it.

Change for the better starts with you and how you communicate with yourself, how you talk to yourself about who you really are and what is possible in your world.

It then ripples out into your everyday interactions with your loved and trusted ones. This local, intimate circle is the necessary rehearsal space, the training ground for Unconditional Communication.

Beyond that we will look at how Unconditional Communication can work to create real change in your workplace, your community, your church, whatever circle you are part of.

And will the Prime Ministers and Presidents and CEOs and Global Principals be changing at the same time as you read this book and ingest its message? Almost certainly not. But you will see, if you like. how conditional their communication is, and how to appropriately disconnect from its worst side-effects.

In the meantime, waiting for The World to change, we change Our World.

We start, right here, right now.

As Václav Havel's poem suggests, if we are ourselves are lost, the whole world and its future will certainly appear lost.

What it takes is for us each to become clear of heart, of vision, and of communication, one at a time.

And then to create, one conversation at a time.

Courage, my friends!

WHAT IS A LEADER?

This book, then, is based on an inside-out approach to change. First you get clear, and then you speak. And that speaking creates something of value to others, out of which comes the desire to create something new. That's the intention of Unconditional Communication.

The world, though, is immersed in outside-in thinking. And usually that means seeking a great leader to come and save us. And too often, we want a new leader to come and punish the previous leader, and all their followers.

So, one last thing, for now, about my issue with 'leadership' as the answer to our prayers.

Much as I understand the constant search for great leadership in our society, I can't help thinking that whenever the word 'leader' is used, there is a hidden assumption that there are 'non-leaders' somewhere close by. And those 'non-leaders' somehow don't have the same capabilities and capacities that 'leaders' do. In the business world, we speak casually about what good leaders can do for and to 'their people.'

This separation is nonsense. We are all made in the same image, and we all have the same capacities for communication
and creation. And we're all doing it all the time.

Let's take a closer look at the meaning of the word leader. Because the origin of the word leader does not mean 'someone
special who will deliver us.'

The etymology of the verb 'to lead' is this:

To lead (v.1)
"to guide," Old English lædan (transitive) "cause to go with oneself;
march at the head of, go before as a guide, accompany and show the
way; carry on; sprout forth, bring forth; pass (one's life)," causative
of liðan "to travel," from Proto-Germanic *laidjanan (source also of
Old Saxon lithan, Old Norse liða "to go," Old High German ga-lidan
"to travel," Gothic ga-leiþan "to go"), from PIE *leit- (2) "to go forth."

Everyone of us has access to that. A leader is someone who
is on a journey - inevitably with self - and almost certainly with others. Sometimes 'going before,' but also always
'accompanying.'

A leader (if you insist on keeping that term) is someone travel-
ing through life, affecting others as they do that.

Oh, you mean like all of us?

All of us the same: with a body and a head, that contains a
brain, and somewhere in there a mind which insists on making sense of everything, constantly making shit up about
stuff. And then trying to convey that sense we've made up to
others.

What Is a Leader?

We are all 'leaders.'

And we all have only communication - whether we use it to break apart, or come together. I want to propose in this book that communication is not one thing, but the only thing. Nothing we are trying to create is going to happen outside the 'ocean of communication in which we all swim.' You don't have many problems or challenges; you have only one. If you transform your communication, you can transform everything.

And, at the same time, none of us are perfect - even those who claim that they are - a myth we encourage every time we try to describe what a great leader would do for us. In the meantime, we all could be better at being human, and every day we get another chance to do better.

Welcome, then, to the human race. We're all stumbling around, making sense of things, trying to make a future happen together. No one's leading this thing, in the old sense of being better equipped or more special than anyone else.

We are all on a journey that is not done yet, and we and the journey are incomplete.

In the face of our incompleteness, I hope we would appreciate all the help we can give each other, and this book is partly about being more helpful with our communication. I believe also that we could all be more sensitive to the fears and vulnerabilities of others. But we must also accept that no-one is coming to save us.

So too, no big leader caused us to be angry and disaffected with one another.

No great leader is going to change what is already in our hearts, whatever else they say or promise. Our heart, and what we express from it, is our business

And no one else can deliver on our own dreams of the future.

I suggest we replace the well-intentioned question

'What does it take to be a great leader?'

with

'What is the best human being I can be?'

And even:

'How powerful a creator can I be?'

Again, change begins with us. This is a book about how every one of us can be the change we want to see in the world. Be the change. Be the creator of the change. As M K Gandhi wrote.

We but mirror the world. All the tendencies present in the outer world are to be found in the world of our body. If we could change ourselves, the tendencies in the world would also change. As a man changes his own nature, so does the attitude of the world change towards him. This is the divine mystery supreme. A wonderful thing it is and the source of our happiness. We need not wait to see what others do.[2]

---

2. 1964, The Collected Works of Mahatma Gandhi, Volume XII

This then is the realization. It's all inside out: the source of everything, including your happiness, is what's going on inside you.

And that capacity to create starts and ends with our Unconditional Communication.

OUR UNCONDITIONAL COMMUNICATION IS WHAT THE WORLD NEEDS

We say, with heartfelt honesty, that we want to create better relationships and bigger futures together. So why do we continue to be disappointed by the results? I propose that it is because we try to do that great work on the foundation of what I call conditional communication. Earlier I have referred to this as 'the old paradigm' of communication: one that values great skills of persuasion in others, and one that makes us into consumers and commentators rather than creators. There is no power – here defined as the capacity to create action - in that paradigm. We need to break that paradigm, however familiar it seems. Because insisting on or accepting conditional communication explains why we don't create what, in our hearts, we know we most want in this world.

So rather than more advice on how to make better relationships and bigger futures based on the wrong, conditional foundations - to continue building on sand, as it were - I want to propose in this book a new paradigm for communication. Deep down, I believe, most of us feel there must be a better way.

Maybe if we start from a different place - a different understanding of what communication is and how it can work - we'll create better outcomes.

So, what is unconditional communication?

We are familiar with the term unconditional in relation to love, support, or surrender.

Unconditional love
Unconditional support
Unconditional surrender

Don't those phrases sound so beautiful, so comforting? Wouldn't you like a bit more of that in the world and in your life?

We know that if something's unconditional, it is absolute. It is pure. It is untainted by expectation of reward. It is not subject to any special terms or conditions. In other words, the love, support, or surrender will happen no matter what else happens.

It will happen because you, and you alone, choose to offer it up in that way. Choice is the key. One of the pillars of unconditional communication is intentionality - being fully aware of when, what, and how we choose to speak, and where we are coming from when we do.

We know, then, that this is the definition of unconditional, even when we know, at exactly the same time, just how crazy difficult that seems to us.

So, what would unconditional communication look like?

Well, what does conditional communication look like? Is it pure and untainted, like Love? No.

Conditional communication thinks about itself first. What's at stake in my conditional communication is me: my self identity. And I need to get something from you to have my communication be successful. As we've seen, if I'm speaking at a conference, I need you to feel I have good content and I've kept you entertained. But communication runs deeper in our identities than that. As social creatures, we have an existential fear of being cast out from the tribe. We'll do what we can to be acknowledged, recognized and valued.

So, conditional communication essentially works on the principle that something has to happen from you in order to make my communication worthy or important or effective. As a result, I am - in other words, 'who I perceive me to be as a valuable member of the human race' - is wholly dependent on your response.

This means you have to acknowledge me or applaud me or give me a high score on the feedback form, or buy my product or service. In other words, you have to act like you're impressed by me. Or you have to act like you are listening to me. You have to understand me, or pretend you understand me. Or you have to act on what I say. You have to go off being inspired. You have to go off and implement something simply because I suggested you might. All these are the conditions I demand in order to keep my self-identity intact and to believe I have been a successful communicator.

But doesn't all that sound great? Doesn't all that sound exactly what we want communication to look like? What's so bad about that?

The trouble is that two things are going on, under the surface of things.

The first thing is that I - as 'the communicator[3]' - am full of expectations about those noble outcomes. I'm full of anxiety about whether my words are going to create my outcomes. So I'm worried about how I'm looking and how I'm sounding, whether I'm getting through to you or whether I am getting it across effectively, and whether I should say different words in a different order. I'm becoming silently obsessed with communication strategies, techniques and styles. I might even be considering changing what I thought I was here to say so that I can get those better outcomes from you. I might be prepared to implement those changes - to 'manage my messaging' - if the result is better or safer, for me.

But deep down, the anxiety comes from my subtle knowing that my communication is conditional, and I know it doesn't feel good.

---

3. One of the things we'll explore is that the distinction between the 'communicator' and the 'communicated to' is in fact unhelpful, since in Unconditional Communication there is no such distinction. But we only have words, so it's a necessary place to start.

Our Unconditional Communication

The second thing going on, in that apparently ideal description of communication, is that you, as my audience, are being anxious about what you are going to do with your response. If you 'get' me, great, we're good! But, in the absence of 'getting me,' what are you going to do with all your not-understanding, not-getting, and not-caring about my communication, all of which might be very real for you?

As audiences in communication, we are often very good at covering all that stuff up. We all know how to look like we are listening. We nod. We smile. We practice 'active listening.' And that's a cover for our anxiety about not 'getting it.' And deep down, that anxiety doesn't feel good.

So our best thinking has gotten us here. All our investment in learning how to be 'good communicators' and all our socialized experiences of being 'well-behaved audiences' has brought us to a place where we all feel anxious about communication.

There has to be a better way.

Unconditional communication is what happens when I speak with you with no concern for my ego's safety. I'll speak full on, without holding back, without dissembling or avoiding. I'll speak that way because **I am not concerned about me - but about YOU, and about us, and about what we could create together.**

Unconditional communication always seeks to create a shared space, whereas conditional communication ultimately always creates separation.

Unconditional Communication

When I love you unconditionally, I love you whether or not you even notice - let alone understand, get or care - that I am loving you unconditionally. I love you unconditionally because I believe and choose it as my highest expression of me being with you. You don't have to do anything in return. But one day, who knows, you might experience it - unconditional love - as something you want to try for yourself.

And if you do, that won't be because of me, it will be that something inside you has woken up.

When I communicate unconditionally, I communicate because what I have to communicate is the best of what I have right now, as my highest expression of me being with you. I am saying these words because I choose, with intention, to say them as the best of what I've got for all of us. You don't have to do anything in return. But one day, who knows, you might experience it as something you want to try for yourself.

And if you do, that won't be because of me, it will be that something inside you has woken up.

Communication is not *from me*, but *inside you*. Communication is not a message I transmit across a void and hope you like it. Communication happens when something that was already there happens inside you.

A metaphor could be helpful here.

Unconditional Communication is Natural

*For just as rain and snow fall from heaven and do not
return without watering the earth, making it bud and sprout,
and providing seed to sow and food to eat, so My word that
proceeds from My mouth will not return to Me empty, but it
will accomplish what I please, and it will prosper where I
send it. You will indeed go out with joy and be led forth
in peace; the mountains and hills will burst into song before
you, and all the trees of the field will clap their hands.*

The Bible, Isaiah 55:10 ff

Water has the entirely natural and seemingly miraculous property of falling from the sky and interacting with the seeds and the fertility of the minerals in the earth and with the warming rays of the sun to instigate new life, bursting forth as fruit and trees and new growth. All that is a process of communication. Something new is born through the water's interaction with what is already waiting for it. The water alone has no power, and nor does the seed. But together?

And the water is still the water, so it rises back up to the sky to be recycled for the next rainfall or snowstorm. It's all a natural, unending cycle.

So too your words have the latent power to generate new thoughts, new imagination, new actions that burst forth, like burgeoning fruit, in your society. Isaiah's text says that God never fails in His words creating exactly what He pleases. We, as humans, have more of a struggle with that. It's more of a stretch goal for us. As humans, we dissemble, we lie, we cheat, we withhold, we try to communicate conditionally. Perhaps we shouldn't be surprised, then, that our words don't always bring about what we intend.

But our words, like the water, still recycle. We don't have a limited amount of words we get to say in our day. They are not draining out through the hole at the front of our head, like a hole in a bucket, all on their way to emptiness.

Tomorrow, you'll get another chance to speak. Your bucket will be full again, with words.

And because today you tried conditional communication and experienced its limited results, maybe tomorrow you won't just open up that hole in the front of your head and let all those words pour out and see what happens. Maybe tomorrow, you'll be more choiceful, more intentional, with your words, and the place they are coming from.

And when your words do, one day, get to make the trees of your fields clap their hands, it will be because your words have tapped into that same, natural, organic, already-there potential that is not just in you, but in everything. Including every audience member you ever communicate with.

Unconditional communication is not about applying techniques to get your point across. It's not a skill. Unconditional communication is more like growing wheat from seed. Innate and natural and dynamic.

Water: not anxious about how it's coming across. Seeds: not anxious about whether they'll sprout in the right way to please the water.

Not from you, but already in everything.

What Unconditional Communication is Not

We've been conditioned to work on our communication so that the 'correct' response happens from our audience. Most communication training is a subtle form of manipulation of others. We are so conditioned into this model that we think the opposite of it must be not achieving anything at all, or speaking like you don't care what occurs.

But unconditional communication is not 'not caring.'

In the world, right now, we have more and more examples of communication that comes in the form of: 'I don't give a shit about what you think, because here's me saying what I want to say!' or 'I can say whatever I want and if you don't like it, then it just shows how wrong you are!' We hear versions of that every day.

And it's a particular form of conditional communication. It's called communicating like a jerk.

Unconditional communication cares deeply about how you respond, but only because your response is a furtherance to the conversation and relationship we are already in and how it might move forward. There's no attachment to a particular, 'right' response. An invitation to one, maybe, if that's what we both choose to accept. But not an attachment to a particular response as a given, as a condition of success.

Unconditional communication might begin with an objective, but is always open to something better and bigger than that being co-created together. Indeed, unconditional communication is actively seeking that new, bigger future.

Unconditional communication knows that any perspective we hold can only ever be partial - no matter how strongly we feel about it. How you will respond is the source of something fresh, and so unconditional communication shows up with humility and curiosity to whatever that might be and whatever might be created from it. Including if your response is 'No.'

Communicating like a jerk is saying 'I want what I say to conquer your own ideas, to obliterate your response, to negate you.' It says my way is the only way, and your acquiescence and compliance is my only goal. Individuals can speak like that, and in our history, whole cultures have acted like that.

Communicating like a jerk is colonialist in nature, and deadly because of that.

'Sticks and stones will break my bones, but names will never hurt me' is a powerful declaration for you to make. But as a statement, it is simply untrue, because it is the names - the words in that statement - that have brought that truth to life for you. Words can be as destructive as any stone. And words can be constructive. There is no 'they are only words.'

What does Unconditional Communication Mean for You?

What if today you were able to communicate unconditionally? Free from any anxiety about how you were coming across or whether people were getting you or whether they liked you or were judging you. Simply feeling free to share what matters most to you.

And because you'd found out what you most wanted to say to the world - as a gift for its bigger future - you stand clear in the possibility that your words might, one day, grow a field of wheat.

What if inspiring others was not down to your skill as a speaker, but instead how your speaking awakens an already-there seed, called 'waiting to be inspired,' in your audience? And that those seeds were all around you, and in everyone?

How do you think you'd show up tomorrow, believing in that possibility?

Because your communication can awaken the potential of others just like the water actuates the seeds. Together.

What does it take? That is what this book is about.

In my professional life, my work involves coaching people.

Sometimes, in our coaching, they end a session inspired, motivated, clear and committed to action.

Sometimes, in our coaching, they get pissed off, upset and tearful.

They prefer the former to the latter, but they can't stop the latter if that's what their life needs them to get.

In both of these scenarios, particularly in the early sessions, my clients think that I am in control of what they get. They make the mistake of thinking, like most of the world in the current paradigm around communication, that I am the cause of their experience. They think that I am inspirational when they are inspired. They think I am a clumsy, rude communicator, when they are upset.

What's really going on is that a seed in them is activated by something going on in the conversation between us. Given I am a nice boy from Yorkshire, England, if it were truly within my control, I'd only deliver happy experiences for them. I'd be a less effective coach overall, because my desire to be liked would divert them from the insights they really needed to get, but my 'personality' would feel better, and my clients would like me more, more consistently. Thankfully, my clients aren't paying me to make me happy.

Coaching doesn't work like that. The seed that gets germinated as insight or realization or 'getting something' does so when it does. Thirty years of coaching and that's the best I can tell you. There is a line in Shakespeare: 'the ripeness is all.' Those of you who are parents will know this. For all your persuasion and urging and loving, and then leaving it alone for a while, and then shouting and threatening, and then more loving, our children get what they need, in terms of growth or insight or breakthrough, exactly when they get it and not before. Whether it's how to tidy up a bedroom or how to get their homework in on time or how to survive a broken heart, the ripeness is, indeed, all.

Really powerful communication has no guarantees, only possibilities. You can't say *this* and always get *that* result. We'd love our communication to be more predictable. We go on courses that promise that. But communication is a lot more real than that. We're not completing a jigsaw here, where one day the final piece will slot into place. We're creating worlds together. And thank God for that.

PART ONE

WHATEVER THE WORLD IS LIKE RIGHT NOW, IT IS CERTAINLY INSIDE OUT AND CO-CREATED

The world doesn't happen to us, but through us.

We are creators. Through our form, the formless comes into being.

In the beginning, there was nothing. The earth was without form, and void.

For God: the void.

For the author: the blank page.

For the actor: the empty stage.

For the artist: the white canvas.

For the entrepreneur with a great idea: nothing as a place to start from, in search of a market.

For the spouse saying 'Yes' to the promise of marriage: an as yet unlived tomorrow to be filled with being married.

In the beginning of anything there is formlessness. Spirit. Consciousness. An idea. An invitation. An intention.

And then some of it gets to be formlessness in form.

Through us.

What is the formless you want to make into form? Love? Joy? Courage? Heart? All of that is going to remain formless unless you find a way to give it form in your communication.

And you do.

Your body, your possessions, your company, your marriage, your children, that favorite mug of yours, that dish they serve at the local Indonesian restaurant, your work - all these are things of form you get to play with in this life.

As humans we get to play with the things of form.

So have fun!

And the single, guaranteed way you'll always have fun is if you keep yourself grounded in the formless from which all of that wonderful formed stuff comes.

Because as soon as you begin to think that the form is the real thing, it will begin to lose its lustre. Its spirit. Its joy. Its aliveness.

Accumulate money for its own sake and it won't deliver what you thought it would. So too with any material possession. Wonderful to have, and have it in full, but know that it is not the essence of what you are craving. Bestbuy.com is a testament to this eternal truth. You can never have enough TVs. There will never be the best TV.

The Dalai Lama tells the story of being invited to an American celebrity's enormous mansion overlooking the Pacific Ocean, and being almost overwhelmed by the beauty and opulence of that home and all the objects within it. And then he talks about going to the bathroom, and inadvertently glancing inside an unclosed vanity cupboard, and seeing bottle after bottle of pharmaceutical medication within it.

So there is the formless.

And then there is the world of form.

Let's not mistake one for the other.

And how great is that, that we all can, and do, create? How great in potential are you and me? Every one of us. Creators.

But what has that got to do with communication? In truth, quite a lot.

Because everything you are trying to communicate is formless:

Your dreams.

Your plan.

Your best qualities.

Your apology.

Your strategy.

Your vision.

Your love.

Your intended marriage.

Your imagined children.

Your health and well-being.

And it will remain formless until you give it form through your Unconditional Communication.

Titles and Subtitles

Titles offer us one of the purest opportunities to enact unconditional communication. They are not orders to be followed, or prescriptions to be fulfilled – they are instead, an invitation to a conversation between reader and author. If you read a title and decide you want nothing to do with the book behind it, that title will not change to better persuade you, it will go on, unconditionally communicating exactly what it intends to communicate. In other words, titles do not require anything of us, they simply are.

The title of this book is Unconditional Communication.

Like the title of any book, it is designed to capture the attention of the prospective reader, even if it has a feeling of mystery to it. 'Unconditional Communication? Huh? What's that about?'

Back in the days of physical bookstores, we authors would think of the title as the thing that caused the browsing customer to pull our book off the shelf, to look at it.

But it is also designed to capture and convey the essence of what I intend to communicate to you, the reader.

The subtitle of any book plays a different and even more important role. It makes a promise. The subtitle says 'read this book about this concept that has captured your attention - and these things will happen.'

So allow me a moment to slow us down and deconstruct the subtitle of this book. What are its key phrases. What am I promising to you, and why?

Bigger Futures

Not better. Bigger.

Better means more of the same. It is a horizontal line of measurement. $1M feels good. Why not go for $2M? That's got to be better, surely? And so the car. And the TV. I own the most substantial, expensive yacht in the world. Until someone else owns a larger, better one.

Bigger, on the other hand, means richer, deeper, more true. Not a horizontal line, but a vertical one.

The horizontal line is about more things of form - achieving things, accumulating things, experiencing things. And, as we've said, as long as that's done in the right spirit, great fun.

The vertical line (and perhaps 'line' is too static a word for the dynamic, moving expansion I'm trying to point to) is about going deeper, about growing. It's about seeking what matters and living in alignment with what we say is the best of us.

It's not about accumulating more form, but an evolvement of the experience of creating out of the formless. It's about achieving alignment with the creator within us.

Bigger is about deeper, richer experiences, rather than more of the same.

It is what Joseph Campbell meant when he said

"People say that what we're all seeking is a meaning for life. I don't think that's what we're really seeking. I think that what we're seeking is an experience of being alive..."

The Lords of Misrule!

Alan and I are taking a break at a gas station on the way to Edinburgh. We are transporting our theater company, The Lords of Misrule, (which, at that time, was just us, Alan and David), and our show, *Gulliver's Travels*, to the Edinburgh Fringe Festival. If you have a theater company, and if you have a show, you have to take them to the Edinburgh Fringe Festival. It is a profound pilgrimage for any artist.

So Alan and I are taking a break at a gas station on the way to Edinburgh, somewhere around Newcastle, about two-thirds of the way to our destination from our starting point in London. It is early evening, and dark already, and it has started to rain.

Tied to the roof of Alan's compact Nissan car is a pile of enormous wooden planks, beams, slats, and hinges that, when taken down and rebuilt, becomes the set of our show. In performance, it becomes, variously, a ship, a flying island, a palace and the set of a glove-puppet show. It's a magnificent experiment in carpentry and engineering. And it works really well for our purposes. We've rehearsed with it for months. We've toured it around England to different theaters, and got great feedback. But right now, in the rain, it looks like an ugly giant, squashing and pummeling Alan's car into the ground.

And Alan, sipping on his coffee, says: 'Do we really need this thing?'

And I say: 'You know, I really don't think we do.'

And so we release it from its bindings, slide it off Alan's car, and drag it behind the gas station's dumpster.

[I apologize now to the dumpster owner, on behalf of The Lords of Misrule. It can't have been a pleasant surprise to find all that wooden junk that next morning.]

Now here's the point of the story.

On any rational level, it was madness to get rid of that contraption. We'd been using it for months, since the very beginnings of *Gulliver's Travels*. We were used to it. It was a central part of the show. It was the first and last thing our audiences saw on stage. We liked it, and our audiences liked it.

It was also madness to dump it, because we were 72 hours away from our first performance of this show to a paying public in Edinburgh. If we threw it away, there'd be nothing there.

But the reason it was so very easy to let that wooden frame go, was because we knew that the source that had created that solid, physical object could just as easily create something else.

We were actors. We were performers.

Long before the English word *actor* came to mean 'act on stage, play the part of,' it meant someone who *makes things happen.*

The English word *performance* comes from a Latin verb meaning *'to accomplish, to form.'*

In other words, our work was to take the formless into form. The formless? The author's words or ideas. The form? Whatever we chose to create.

And that connection to the source that makes authors' ideas and words into characters and situations on a stage, for the benefit of the audience who would be moved, touched, and inspired by what was made into form. What of that?

That connection is unending...and the source of that creativity is without end.

That was our faith as actors.

We had decided, in the past, to make a thing of form in wood and iron.

And we could throw it away because we knew, as a certainty, that the creativity would always be there to make something new.

For those who like the endings to stories, Alan and I did create something else. Nothing. We decided to do a show without any set at all. We decided to rely on our own ability to convey a ship, a flying island, a palace and the set of a glove-puppet show. We decided to rely on our audience to co-create those things in their imaginations, because we knew their imagination was more powerful than any material construction. And that year, we won the Fringe First Award in Edinburgh.

Here is the good news.

You have access to that source of creation also. It is simply not true that Alan and I had access to that source because we were Actors - and you can't because you are, for example, an introvert.

You just need to get out of your own way to access the same source. What would that look like? Well, you could stop calling yourself names. Whenever you say 'I'm not creative' or 'I don't have it in me' or 'I am too busy' or 'I have too many responsibilities to do what I really want' - these are sticks and stones that are breaking your creative bones. The thing about using language like this on ourselves is that we think we are being descriptive. The danger is that we come predictive. The danger is we believe ourselves. 'I am not creative' becomes 'And I'll never be creative.'

Let's explore more of how to access this space.

The rehearsal room for theater people is a place of joyous, playful creativity.

It is also a sacred space. Actors gather there with a faith in the process. They take it seriously, for all its fun. They give it the reverence that making the invisible visible deserves.

One of the things you experience as an actor is that you are in a position of privilege.

When you are being asked to be a channel for Shakespeare, Swift, or Beckett, you don't take that honor lightly. Because you are not just the channel for Shakespeare, Swift, or Beckett, great as those writers were, but for the creativity that they, in their turn, were channels for.

And where does *that* come from?

That's a big question, and so you approach it with a due degree of humility. Even though, come the closing curtain, the audience is going to be applauding you and your fellow performers, you know it is really not much about you at all. You are merely standing at the front of a line of formless becoming form, currently being passed on through you.

But you do have a part to play in that creation. Just as spiritual gurus sit and meditate for hours to let the Truth come through them, so you, as an actor, do your best to prepare. Most of all, that looks like staying loose, moving the body. Go backstage before a performance, prior to the audience being let into the auditorium, and you will see actors rolling about on the stage, leaping up and falling down, throwing their voices around like so many fishing lines being cast out into limitless streams.

Because relaxation aids the flow of creativity. Letting go of tension grows communication.

That is the same for all of us...and what most gets in the way, for most of us, is the mind.

"I am not creative. What if they judge me? What if it all goes wrong? What if I am caught out?

That mind chatter, for creative expression, is like stepping on a garden hose for the water - it impedes the flow.

That's why my work in communication with people begins with calming the mind. No amount of tips and techniques will help if the mind is raging with doubt and insecurity, or even mis-placed certainty. No training in skills will work if the mind is telling us we don't really want to be here at all.

So, slow down.

Relax.

Calm yourself.

Be at peace.

That's the foundation for Unconditional Communication.

So, communication is the process of bringing formless into form.

Theatre being manifested through performers.

Consciousness becoming form through human life.

God, in the Bible stories, becoming form through Jesus the carpenter.

Products and services becoming form through organizations

Money being created through our work.

Our personal growth becoming manifest through our actions.

Relationships becoming rich and rewarding through our behaviors.

Formless into form.

This is the game we are all playing. Or rather, the game that is being played through us.

I haven't been on a theater stage, as an actor, since 1994.

But now I glimpse it every time I begin a new book.

The blank page. Waiting for the words to appear.

Just like the empty stage, waiting for the creation of worlds.

So the first foundation of Unconditional Communication is accepting yourself as a creator. And a creator of Bigger Futures for you and others. You stop calling yourself names that limit and belittle you. You start acknowledging and recognizing and celebrating all the things you have created already in your life. That relationship (even if it ended). That car (even if you had to sell it). That project at work (even if it didn't work out like you wanted in the end). That child (even if they think you're stupid right now).

Unconditional Communication starts with what you want to create in the world. And, at the same time, as soon as you've declared that, you find that it's not all about you, and can never be all about you.

Better Relationships

That Bigger Future is only going to be created with and through others in your life.

It's all *co*-created.

The quality of the relationships you create is the catalyst for the bigness of the future you make for you and others.

As an actor, the first true lesson you learn is that you are a creator of worlds, and you better take that role with the right amount of gravitas and humility.

The second true lesson you learn as an actor is that you aren't doing that work alone.

I am not Gulliver because I act that I am. I am Gulliver because I act that I am, and you agree to believe that I am.

Acting is not a solo act of skill and competence.

Acting is a social, co-creative agreement.

And so is all communication.

Until my audience agrees to play their part in creating me as Gulliver, I am a sad, sweating man in a cheap costume speaking words that are not his own.

But if we can, together, get past that, we can create worlds together. We can see things that aren't actually there. We can be moved and inspired. Back in the days of The Lords of

Misrule, our audiences didn't laugh and cry - and they did - because they were overwhelmed by our brilliance as actors. They laughed and cried because they saw something that was true *for them*.

There's an old lesson from communication training: *know your audience*. Most people have no idea what that really means. They get side-tracked by trying to anticipate their audience, to predict their preferences and habits. To accumulate facts about their audience.

To the actor, *know your audience* means 'Without them, I will simply not exist.'

'Know your audience' is a stance toward the wellbeing and success of your audience - not an accumulation of data about them. The former is an aspect of love, the latter is a form of stalking.

In any communication, we need to have a profound respect for our audience, not as passive recipients of our message, but as active co-creators of our futures with us.

What if we all treated each other as if we were all actively involved in creating our preferred and best outcomes together? All had the seed of potential inside us, waiting to be activated?

How would Presidents and Prime Ministers speak to their citizens?

How would bosses speak to their employees?

How would parents speak to their children?

How would teachers speak to their students?

Not communicating to, but communicating with.

And I am inviting you now to go beyond what you think I might be saying. Because this is not just about being more respectful to our audiences, or paying them more of the attention they deserve because they are co-creators of any communication with us.

I want you to know that the separation that we believe is a given of reality is, in truth, an illusion.

Loneliness: the Generation Z Epidemic

When I speak about this separation, I am pointing to a way that we habitually see the world. Loneliness is one symptom of that separation, and apparently, it is becoming more widespread.

For all the diverse communication channels that promise being connected in our world,

a survey of 20,000 U.S. adults ages 18 and older found that almost half report feeling alone (40%) or left out (47 %). One in four (27 %) feel they are not understood. Two in five (43 %) feel relations are not meaningful and they feel isolated (43%). Generation Z (those born after about 1995) was found to be the loneliest generation.[4]

---

4. Cigna's survey, 2018, based on the UCLA Loneliness Scale

Loneliness is a state of emotional and spiritual suffering—the pain of feeling separate and disconnected. Frank J. Ninivaggi M.D., commenting on this research, suggests:

Loneliness emanates from the mind's intrinsic default tendency toward irreparable splitting into twos.

And it is all an error of perception.

Look at The Mountains!

I'm with a group of 45 executives in a meeting room in a hotel in Switzerland. The room has huge, floor-to-ceiling windows which means that we have uninterrupted views of the stunningly beautiful Alps.

I ask the 45 executives to stand up and turn to the windows. I ask them to look at the mountains.

Then I ask them: 'Where exactly are the mountains?'

A number of them take the easy bait and raise their hands to point. 'Out there!' they say.

And where else are the mountains when you look at the mountains?

Think about it. Or rather, don't think about it. Experience it. Put down this book and have a look now at whatever is outside your own nearest window. What's there as you look? A car? An office block? A tree? Are they truly only 'over there'?

And where are you, who is looking at the mountains? Are you 'here,' separate from the mountains, the car, the office block, the tree?

No.

You are never separate.

There is no you 'over here' looking at the mountains 'over there.' You and the mountain and the you being aware of looking at the mountain are all arising in the same shared space, in the same living dynamic. You, the mountains, the awareness of you looking at the mountains are all in the same space called your mind. Or you might call it your imagination. Or your awareness.

And that's the same for every one of us.

And therefore, you and I looking at each other are not two separate objects in distinct spaces.

We are all in the same shared space.

Try it right now. Where is me, David, writing, and where are you, reading?

I am inside your mind, and you are in mine.

Exactly how much more connected do you want to be to other people?

Our separateness from each other is a mind-made illusion.

All appears through us – our thoughts, of course, our sensations of being in our body, yes, and then, in fact the whole world. Everyone in it, what other people are doing around and to us, this trash can beneath the table, all the beautiful mountains, this apple in my hand. All a part of our awareness.

All there ever is, is awareness, occurring through you.

That everything in our experience appears through us is one of the most extraordinary realities, and we take it so much for granted that we do not notice it. Ironically, we are often unaware of our awareness. But if we relax enough to observe what's going on, we can see its Truth.

Your mind - as we will see in the next chapter - hates the reality of this true connection and tries always to create a distance between us. In this case, your mind is not your best friend.

Everything in the paradigm of conditional communication is built on the illusion that we are separate. All the strategies of conditional communication are about overcoming an apparent gap between us: that you don't get me or understand me or know me, and I need to do something to overcome that deficiency. That's why we have been trained to communicate to try to be impressive, or strong, or smart, or even attractive - because we believe those things close the gap. But there isn't a gap.

How would we communicate if we knew we were already, always connected?

Maybe, at the very least, we'd be less anxious.

Maybe, if I always knew, when I communicate with you that, I was going to end up in your mind, I'd decide to take care in there. I'd take my boots off at the door. I'd tread lightly. I could get curious about how your mind works, different from mine. I could wander your mind's corridors and see how all that accumulated experience and belief systems have brought you to believe what you think. Just as I tend always to believe what I think.

You can call this empathy or emotional intelligence. But it's certainly about showing up as a friend in each others' minds, rather than as a clumsy stranger, or a warrior.

Now I can see that this 'other, separate' person is not wrong to my right, but right as well as I am. The only sane question to ask is not 'How can I change their mind?' but 'What could we choose to create together, given what we both believe?'

This is the Golden Rule: communicate with others as you would have them communicate with you.

I can have strong convictions, and let them be strong convictions, but also choose not to be loud about them. My Dad never liked Woody Allen. But he didn't wander around looking for opportunities to tell people why. He didn't want to create a Facebook Group about it.

Maybe, as well, if we knew we were already, always connected, we'd be more conscious of our own mind at play, and how that mind might be a help or a hindrance when it comes to shaping our communication.

Because how the mind is operating is part of where we are coming from when we create what we create. Our mind can insist that you are 'Other,' and we let it. Or the mind can relax into connection, and we allow it.

Where I am coming from in my communication is foundational to what then gets created. If I come from anxiety, my communication is likely to be hesitant and unclear, and that will create frustration between us. If I come from a place of judgement, no matter what I say, the person in the relationship with me will sense that, and become defensive in turn.

My friend is talking about a difficult conversation she's just had with her business partner. She highlights a particular moment - a word that was said - when all the pent up emotion came flowing out, on both sides, and some hurtful things were said. 'That's the moment the conversation went south,' she says. I ask her to wonder if it was always going to go south, not because of that particular moment, but from before the conversation even began. From the place she was coming from before it started. From the place where she believed there was a dangerous gap.

When I am faced with a difficult conversation and I start with a gap, I am always going to be made anxious by that. I am going to reach for strategies. I'm going to look up 'how to do it' on the internet. I am going to rehearse my arguments in advance and then see how that goes in reality.

Or I could come from a place of curiosity. I could start by asking how they feel and how they are thinking about this situation, rather than waiting to see how soon I can unleash my needs and demands. I could start from realizing that my own needs and demands - which feel so urgent to me - can only be partial versions of the truth in this situation. I could see if we can develop, together, a best possible result for both of us, and then ask what we could each do, or stop doing, to allow that to happen.

Intentionality is crucial in this work. We get to choose how we speak and where we come from when we speak. Or we can continue to speak automatically and robotically, come from our instincts and conditioned responses. And how is that working for us?

So 'Better Relationships' is a key phrase in this book's subtitle. Because relationships are channels for something.

A relationship is a channel for love, for intimacy, for fun, for children, for success.

An organization - a network of relationships - is a channel for purpose and service.

The word communication, in its language origins, means 'sharing meaning together.'

Influence, in its language origins, means 'flowing together as one.'

It is the mind that creates the separation we are so frightened of. We should be more angry with Ratty than we are. But that's for the next chapter.

In the meantime, there is one more element in this book's subtitle. Together.

Together

Unconditional Communication is transformational because it accesses the power of the whole, the collective.

We need Unconditional Communication because we need to move our world from a series of 'Us & Them' tribes to a collective 'We, Together.'

And our communication needs to be able to deliver that.

Unconditional Communication doesn't say my communication is good because you are moved to give me 12 out of 10 on a feedback form.

It says the communication we can create through relationships with each other is a sign of our co-dependent, co-creative reliance on each other. And that realization of our co-dependence is the foundation of shared commitment.

There has to be something bigger than any leader's ego - no matter how compelling that might appear - and that is 'What all of us together can create.'

All of us are smarter than any one of us.

Unconditional Communication may say:

> 'I have a story to share - and I now have
> ways of sharing it more effectively'

but it also says:

'Unless we - me and you the audience - live this story
out, nothing of value is going to happen. I am not
communicating *about* something, I am communicating *so
that* something. I as speaker am a servant of you the audience
and our bigger collective future. I am not in control, but we -
together - may find a way to be in control of our destiny.'

Mary Parker Follett (1868 - 1933) was a pioneer in thinking
about any organization - business or society - being a function
of its collective well-being and participation. She said it well:

*That is always our problem, not how to get control of people,
but how all together we can get control of a situation.*

Co-creation is not a nice next step for business or a community to take: it's the nature of the universe. An atom can't do
it alone. A cell can't be a muscle. A synapse can't be in charge
of the brain.

The internet and social media has flowered at this stage of
human development to show us the truth of this. The internet, even Facebook, is an expression of collective will. As early
adopters, we are still using it in pretty shallow and dysfunc-
tional ways, but we have time to grow into its potential.

Having the whole of human knowledge at our fingertips has
not been the holy grail, as we'd been promised: we still are
faced with how we apply that knowledge together.

Being able to connect with everyone on the planet has not
produced heaven on earth; we are currently too distracted by
funny cat videos and toxic debate.

But the truth is there: there is no CEO of the internet; there is no leader (in the old sense of that term) of social media.

The whole thing works by invitation ('Here's my Google Document about something that matters to me - would you like to join?') and collaboration.

If you want a simple sign that someone is coming from a place of Unconditional Communication, you'll see much more invitation and much less persuasion at play. You'll experience being in a place of curiosity and discovery with them than an experience of their certainty.

The internet will, in time, become the shared space where we can create Bigger Futures and Better Relationships, Together, across the planet.

In the meantime, we can practice it in our local 'real' worlds.

From One to Many

In this book, I'm going to look at communication mostly in terms of your connection with others in your world, whether that be at the level of friendship, intimate relationship, neighbourliness or the workplace (it's all the same and not different).

At the end of the book, however, I am going to suggest that there are ways of communicating unconditionally that can transform our public discourse. We've conditioned ourselves, as it were, into conditional communication being the default at the interpersonal level. I believe there is a huge cost to have that conditionality being at the heart of our collective conversations.

So, before I end this book, I'm going to suggest that we can move beyond our current structures of debate, interview and Town Hall - and into processes that reflect our desire to participate in and shape our collective futures. Because we are not at our best when we are consumers of others' promises and policies. We have so much more wisdom, talent and commitment to share than that.

I'll talk about methodologies like Open Space - and the other practices like it that come under the umbrella of 'emergent' or 'self-organizing principles.' These approaches work, but not because they teach people *about* how important co-creation is. We don't need to have an introduction to the theory first, so we can understand the expertise of the design. We don't even need to get into a state of loving-kindness before we start. We just leap in.

These methodologies, I repeat, are not about co-creation, they *embody* co-creation. They allow and encourage co-creation to happen in the moment. They allow participants to experience themselves as co-creators - without them even needing to know how or why it is working in that way. Indeed, rather than needing to train or develop collaboration skills, these approaches simply allow them to emerge. These approaches trust that the seed of collaboration is already there, waiting to be activated. We get to remember just how natural and human it is to connect, and to create something wonderful together.

More on this, later.

In the meantime, thank you for being on this journey together with me, on the upward spiral.

PART TWO

THE UPWARD SPIRAL

The central image for Unconditional Communication is the upward spiral.

Because that's what life looks like. It's how life is wanting to move.

Life is interested in rising up - through stages of development, through technological advancement, through more evolved, inclusive ways of organizing businesses or societies, and through higher levels of individual consciousness - from fear, for example, to love.

Life looks up.

Life is also interested in expanding, gathering new experiences and expressions, including the best of what went before, discarding what no longer works. Life includes and transcends, moves through everything we feel, think, and do – every boundary we break – every obstacle we overcome – every insight we glean.

Ever upward, ever outward.

The Circle of Life is not, in fact, a circle, but an upward spiral.

Your life is like that too, as long as you live it consciously. Close up it can have bumps and barriers, and they are very real. But if you pull back for the longer view, for all its pains and problems, you'll see that your life is moving up and out. It is moving in an upward spiral.

There are three energies that cause the spiral to rise.

1.   Presence
2.   Connection
3.   Created Outcomes.

PRESENCE

They say that Ayrton Senna - the Formula 1 driver who died in 1994 - had a presence that could stop a room.

Bill Clinton once told the story of being at a party when suddenly the energy of the room shifted to the door. Bill Clinton, no mean celebrity (this was before he became President), and a pretty compelling human being in his own right, was probably used to having most of the attention on him. But when he turned to see where all the energy was drawn, he saw that David Letterman had walked in.

I was once in the same airport lounge as Angelina Jolie in Heathrow. I found it difficult to take my eyes off her, mostly because how focused she was on her two children. It was almost as if there was a glass dome over the space she was in with them, and no other person was in the lounge, especially not staring strangers like me.

Presence means nothing in the way. Nothing at all. No expectation, neediness, desire, fear or anxiety.

I am Ayrton Senna and I am really, really here, and I walk into a room and the room stops. I am Ayrton Senna and I have no urge to make the room stop or hope that it will...In fact, I may not even notice that it does when it does. Because I am present only to being here, not how my being here will impact others.

Presence of this purity is as rare as rocking horse shit. And that it is why it is so compelling for others. They don't get to be around it very often. They get to be around leaders who are keeping something back, or have a hidden agenda, or are just trying too hard to be really cool. None of that is in the same universe as presence[5].

---

5. And there are dangers here. How many spiritual leaders have fallen from grace in sexual scandals? Here's what I think is going on there. I think their spiritual practice developed their capacity for being - in the old hippy saying - here, now. They didn't develop that so that they could have more sex; but then they found that their presence was becoming attractive - in the sense of energetically magnetic - to others. And at that point both they and their followers were faced with what to do with that attraction. And too often, they all fell. From a place of 'here, now', to 'have sex, now'.

Your own presence will rise when three internal statements are true for you:

One: I want to be here.

Two: I am happy to be here.

Three: I am here.

Try these internal statements out when you are next in a situation where you want to find out if you are present or not.

I am changing my baby's nappy. He has had explosive diarrhea and it has filled the diaper and shot up his back. There are stains over clothes, bedsheets, bodies and hands.

And at this point I ask myself:

Do I want to be here?

Am I happy to be here?

And: am I here?

Knee deep in baby poop, am I really, truly, happily here?

If I am, I am. The circumstance has nothing to do with it. I won't be more present when the baby's nappy is changed and I am relaxing in front of the TV with a glass of wine. Unless I am. I'm only ever present now, or I am not.

People say to me, how do I increase my presence, David?

To which the answer is 'You don't. You get rid of what's in the way of your being here. Your presence - my presence - our presence - is the natural state. It's the default. Your baby is really present, even when covered in poo. Your dog also, is an embodiment of presence.

What takes you away from that level of presence - what drags you away from that Heaven into the Hell of separation - is the workings of your mind.

I shouldn't be here.

I don't deserve to be here.

It's someone else's fault that I am here.

I don't agree with why I have to be here.

These circumstances don't allow me being present.

All that trash. All that internal dialogue, all that mind chatter.

Your baby doesn't have that mind yet. Your dog never will.

You, on the other hand, are cursed with a mind, and you have two options:

1. If it is really true you shouldn't be here, then you shouldn't be here. Go. Stop explaining yourself to me. Just go, and be clean with going. That would be committing to more presence than you have right now. Or

2. Stop paying attention to that mind chatter; stop making it strong by telling it how sensible and accurate it sounds. Let it go. Think of it like listening to someone having a nightmare in the hotel room next to you. You can hear it acting itself out through the thin walls, but you don't have to be in the same nightmare yourself.

How to be here

Put your hand on the table in front of you. Look at your hand.

Look more.

While you are looking at your hand, your mind will begin to chatter.

"What the heck is this exercise about? Why I am looking at my hand? I am so busy. I am so much smarter than whatever this exercise if about. Wow, look at those nails. They need cutting!"

Don't connect to any of that chatter. It's not really yours. It's happening in the hotel room next to you.

Now relax your looking.

And now you can look at your hand anew.

Look at it. On the table. Just being there.

Your hand is fully present at being a hand on the table. And there is nothing else in the way of that.

If you stay with that looking long enough, you'll begin to feel the same presence as your hand has. Because presence is magnetic.

But you'll only experience that when you get tired of paying so much attention to your own mind chatter.

And when that mind chatter has begun to release its hold on you, then you'll begin to become more present to the presence of your hand, simply being a hand on the table.

And now, when you really get into that state, you can look up from the hand on the table and transfer that gaze to someone or something else.

And still be present.

There is a difference between 'presence' and 'trying to be present'.

At the heart of it is this is the idea that if there is any effort or energy dispelled in *being present*, and it causes us to be exhausted because of this effort, then that is not presence at all.

This truly is something that I cannot explain as a concept or that you will get as a purely intellectual understanding. It's something you have to experience for yourself. Begin by noticing those moments - short or long - when you notice that you are really here. And how it feels.

As we have seen, presence occurs when three internal statements are true:

One: I want to be here.

Two: I am happy to be here.

Three: I am here.

Being present starts with listening inwardly. One of the ways that we grow into being present is by learning to listen or be aware of the alternative statements that appear to be true in our mind when we are wanting to be present.

This week, try and become aware of what statements are going through your head when you notice that you want to be present.

When you voice the 'presence statement' I want to be here...

What comes up as thought in opposition to that?

When you voice: I am happy to be here....

What comes up as thought in opposition to that?

When you voice: I am here...

What comes up as thought in opposition to that?

The practice, ultimately, is not to argue and bargain with those alternative voices. The practice is to let them go, so that they lose their volume and insistency. When it comes to our mind, we confuse insistency and repetition with accuracy. When it comes to the mind, we think the mind must be telling us the truth because it is so goddamn loud and familiar.

That is an error of judgment.

If I have something in my head, I don't have to listen to it

Or I can speak it out to remove its hold on me. I can let it speak, and then I can ask: is that true? Is that statement real? Is it useful? How does it serve me?

Hello Everyone, please meet Ratty and Angelo!

And at this point, as a way of trying to become more aware of the internal dialogue, let me introduce you to Ratty and Angelo.

In my workshops, I draw Ratty as a cartoon rat's head with pointy ears, black nostrils, sharp whiskers and little red eyes.

Angelo I draw as a faceless, sexless angel with big wings and a flowing robe.

Ratty is the name I gave to the internal voice which always seems to be chattering away in the background. Sometimes we are very aware of that internal chatter. This is particularly true at times of anxiety, which explains why I started using Ratty and Angelo in my early presentation skills work.

Many people, at the beginning of their experience of presentations or public speaking, are afraid. When I introduce the cartoon of Ratty, and ask them if they know what I am talking about, they don't say Yes. They say YES!!!

Ratty always has an explanation for what we are experiencing. He's full of stories. Unfortunately many of those stories have a negative tinge, whether he might be saying something bad about us – "You should've prepared more for this meeting!!" - or about others - "Senior executives don't really care about you!"

Ratty can get particularly loud and virulent when people like me suggest that you might not want to listen to Ratty all the time. He says 'This guy David is an idiot; why would you trust him over my familiar voice?'

The power and the problem of Ratty is that he is extremely persuasive. When he talks it always sounds like he's telling us the truth of the matter. Ratty is one of the best, most effective communicators you will ever encounter. One proof of that statement is that you always, always want to believe him.

The opportunity, however, is to realize that Ratty is not you.

Ratty is just a part of you, one voice among others. Discernment is the key.

I happen to believe that Ratty is the ego, I believe Ratty is that thing you call 'me' - a conditioned psychological reality called 'I'.

In the world of form, our 'I's' and 'Me's' are kept separate from each other. No one else has your Social Security Number, so how can we be all together and not separate? Ratty's job inside you is to reinforce your disconnection from others - and to make that a fraught and risky experience. And why does he do that? Because Ratty knows that he will die - go silent forever - when you know how to truly connect with others.

But we've no need to get sidetracked by my philosophy here. I just want to know if the actual experience is true for you too. Do you hear Ratty chattering and is that chatter annoying or even disempowering? I know that Ratty sounds sensible and helpful - that's one of his greatest gifts - but exactly how helpful, in your lived experience, is your Ratty voice?

Now Angelo. Angelo is not your sports coach standing on the touch lines screaming "Come on, you, you can do it!"

Angelo is the opposite of Ratty in a much more significant way. While Ratty is the voice of interpretations & stories about experience, Angelo simply tells the truth of the experience.

So if I'm doing a presentation and someone walks out of the room, Ratty is likely to say 'There you are David; I told you that you hadn't prepared enough! People are finding you so boring they want to leave!'

Angelo simply says 'People walk out of rooms.' Because that is true. And that doesn't need to mean anything else.

Angelo is there to bring us back to a place of being present, of being aware of what is, before our stories begin to make all that mean something.

Angelo brings us back to calm, and peace, and the source of all creation. Whereas Ratty is the source of all reaction.

There can come great freedom when we realize that Ratty is not the only voice in our head. We can take some control as to who we listen to.

After all, who is the voice saying 'Ah, I noticed that Ratty is speaking; I wonder what he's trying to say this time and should I bother to listen?'

The voice noticing Ratty can't be Ratty. Who is that voice?

And who is the voice saying 'Angelo is returning me to a place of no stories, a place where I can trust myself and create from. Thank you Angelo.'?

I'd suggest that voice is coming from the place of Presence.

Ratty would have you believe that it's more like Absence. He wants to insist that his voice is right. He tells you that unless you try really hard to keep guessing what other people are thinking - like he does - then you'll revert to a form of relaxation where you won't notice anything at all. And in all that, Ratty sucks you into a drama that's most likely only happening in your own mind.

One of the secrets is that you don't *get to* presence. You *get back* to it, by turning down the volume on Ratty.

Ratty wants to tell you that something is wrong. Something is wrong with the situation. Or something is wrong with the people you are communicating with. Ultimately, Ratty is implying (though he wants to be your friend, so he wouldn't ever say this out loud) that there is something wrong with you.

There was a popular book on human psychology in the 1960s. It is called 'I'm OK; You're OK.'

It said, in short: 'You can't build anything of value unless you *know* that you are OK.'

Ratty would die if he knew you were truly OK. He depends on your weakness. That's why he continues to undermine you.

And human beings are energetic creatures: they transmit energy. When you show up as not OK, consciously or subconsciously, your audiences will pick up on that. They'll sense, at some level, that you are not OK. That something is wrong. That will feed their own Rattys: 'I knew I shouldn't have come to this meeting.'

Aryton Senna enters the room from a place of nothing is wrong. I'm OK, you're OK. And it is so unusual, so rare, it stops the room.

Presence is fun

I think more people would be more present more consistently if they allowed themselves to experience how wonderful an experience being present is. It feels good to be free of Ratty. There's an energy to it. There's a lightness to it. There's a vitality to it. People smile when they are present. It's fun!

Eckhart Tolle. Funny guy. Adyashanti. Funny guy. Ram Dass. Funny guy.

Politicians and TV evangelists trying to be funny? Not funny. Creepy. Because their communication doesn't arise from

Presence - unconditionality - but from a desire to look good – i.e. conditionality. They want to be funny because they've heard somewhere that being funny will make them more human. When in fact trying to be funny makes them less human and more robotic.

True presence is fun. But not many people allow themselves to get there very often.

They tell me how hard it will be to stop being so busy, to stop all those Ratty thoughts. It's hard, David. I have things to do, people to see. I have distractions.

On one level, people don't like the idea of slowing down in this way. Their currency is time and a lot of time could be wasted from being Present, they think. Better to stay with what's familiar: the anxiety of being busy.

I think they are anxious of hearing what Angelo is trying to say, if they stopped to be Present. The sound and fury of our daily lives is a good way to drown out the insistent voices calling us to be more present. Being busy is a great distraction from the truth of our experience.

I would be more myself, if I wasn't so busy.

I would be a better me, if I didn't have these urgent responsibilities.

I could be capable of greatness, but in the meantime I have stuff to get done.

PART TWO

Who knows what amazing things they could generate from being fully Present more? To go back to the source of all creation.

But in the meantime, they're busy.

"Why, This is Hell, Nor am I Out of It." Who Said That?

It's fun to be close to the peaceful reality of Presence, of All That Is. And it's a nightmare to be separated from it.

I was brought up to see Hell as somewhere 'down there,' where all the torments of all the damned are repeated forever in a place of fire. Later in life, I came across Dante's frozen wasteland, where the traitors were held, in damnation, locked forever in a lake of ice. No vitality ever again. No movement. No joy.

And then, at High School, I read Christopher Marlowe's play based on the Dr Faustus myth. Doctor Faustus is an extremely intelligent scholar at the University of Wittenberg. And he is remorseless in his ambition. And he's made the biggest mistake of all: that more of the things of form will get him what he is seeking. He doesn't want Bigger Futures, he seeks Better Futures i.e. more knowledge, more insight, more access to secret teachings[6]. And so, in the play, he agrees to sell his soul to the Devil in return for that betterment.

---

6. Dr Faustus would be in BestBuy every day!

41

I always had one favorite scene in Marlowe's play. Doctor Faustus has, he thinks, summoned the Devil, Lucifer, but instead finds himself in conversation with one of the Devil's disciples, Mephistopholis:

Faust. *And what are you that you live with Lucifer?*

Meph. *Unhappy spirits that fell with Lucifer,*
Conspir'd against our God with Lucifer,
And are for ever damn'd with Lucifer.

Faust. *Where are you damn'd?*

Meph. *In hell.*

Faust. *How comes it then that thou art out of hell?*

Because, like me in my mistaken youth, Faustus thinks Hell is a place. A location. Down there. And since Mephistopholis is here in Faustus's study, he can't be somewhere else, in that other place called Hell.

To which comes Mephistopholis' shocking reply:

Meph. *Why this is hell, nor am I out of it.*
Think'st thou that I who saw the face of God,
And tasted the eternal joys of Heaven,
Am not tormented with ten thousand hells,
In being depriv'd of everlasting bliss?

Why this is hell, nor am I out of it. Now I get it! Hell is the place you are in forever when God has cast you out of his Presence.

When you only have form around you, and when you have disconnected from the source of the form.

My Dad taught me, as a boy, that Hell was a place Down There, and Heaven was a place Up There. It's easier for young minds to take things literally.

And how do I translate that now? Hell is not a place. It's a state of being. Hell is the condition of not being present, right here, right now.

When you are trapped in the world of form and have no access to the brilliance of the formless, that's hell. And it's down there, near the bottom of what you might call the ladder of consciousness. Fear, anger, shame, complaint.

Being disconnected is fearful.

Being fully present is the foundational place of calm, peace and confidence, out of which we can begin to create something of value with others.

That's why the second path of Unconditional Communication is Connection.

CONNECTION

As often as I can when I visit London, I go and see my friend Neil Mullarkey perform with his improvisation group The Comedy Store Players.

I find it belly-laugh-out-loud funny.

I also find it deeply moving.

Six people helping each other out. Making something out of – literally – nothing. Doing it for each other for the joy of their art – and doing it in the service of their audience, who will be transported for two hours out of the world of constrained form and into the limitless space of formlessness.

Work as love made visible. 15.00 GBP, 7.30pm Sundays and Wednesdays.

Go and observe it. It's magical. And fun. And shows what can be created from being fully present in a place of connection.

It's Not All About You: Communication as an act of Service

Improvisation fails as soon as one performer makes it all about them. No matter how temporarily funny or smart they look, what is lost to us is the power of co-creativity: something bigger than any of us.

Improvisation works on subsuming the ego for the benefit of the whole, of the greater good. There's no lead role, no small roles either. Instead, six people work in unison to create a collective and collaborative performance. Even the audience has a part to play, by providing suggestions and ideas, in co-creating this new reality.

The performers ask for inputs from the audience, out of which they will create a sketch.

Unconditionally marks this whole communication. The performers say 'Give us your ideas, and we'll say Yes to whatever they are, and make something up from it.'

The audience says 'An aardvark.' Or 'Film Noir.' And at the same time they are saying 'Take this idea and see what you can do with it.'

No-one is constrained by conditions of what is supposed to happen. Whatever happens will be good.

I think that is why there is so much laughter in the room. It's not just that these performers are skilled in being funny. I think the laughter is a joyful reaction to the realization that none of us knows that is going to happen next. And that feels good.

So too, communication is not about getting your point across or impressing someone or showing you are the smart one, but communication is about serving the needs of your audience. In The Comedy Store, the improvisation arises out of a dynamic, unconditional sharing and intermingling of needs.

We'll explore what I mean by that and how it will be critical to you a little later. But I'd like to approach it first with a different metaphor: all communication is a conversation.

And I don't mean that when you communicate that you should be conversational ie relaxed, natural, chatty. Although that is something good to aspire to.

[...compared with communication that sounds like 'corporate speak' or 'presentation talk' (eg, 'Thus it can be seen on the next slide that...'). Or communication that sounds like a lecture (in good or bad senses!).

Or communication that exploits a power differential (I know more than you, I have authority over you and you have to comply, and so on). I'm sure we've all had experiences of hearing communication that is like that - stilted, forced, un-natural - not really human - yes? It's creepy.]

But when I say that 'all communication is a conversation' I mean that quite literally all communication causes there to be a conversational response. It is the way human minds work.

It's happening right now. I state: Conversation is the way human minds work.

And what happens? There's a response. In you. And where does that response happen? In your mind.

There was a statement, and a statement in response.

When I first said a moment ago that 'all communication is a conversation' - you instantly responded in your mind. You might have responded 'Wow, that's fascinating!' or 'Huh? So what?"

We are in a conversation. If you were listening to me say this at a conference, that same conversation would be emerging, even though the security cameras recording our interaction would only ever show that one person was doing any speaking out loud. And in this book, I am the person typing out these words, but you are still having a conversational response to it.

So we might consider all communication as the aspiration to hold powerful conversations together.

What if we didn't plan our communication from the starting point of 'What will I say and how will I say it?'

but

'What creative conversation do I want my audience to have with me through the course of the communication - and how can I engage with them to bring that about?'

and

'What conversations are my audience already having about me and my subject before I open my mouth - and what do I need to consider to work with that?'

and

'How do I address my audience's need around this topic so that they can be more present to the conversation I'd like to explore with them?'

There is something called Conversational Noise. That's the conversation you are having in your head about me or my subject that drowns out what I am saying.

What are the most common conversations audiences have in their heads when this noise is present?

"What's this about?"

or

"What's this got to do with me?"

or

"What's this person got up their sleeve?"

Now, why would you ever be asking those questions in your head?

Because those questions matter to you.

They are needs that are not being satisfied.

And until those needs are met, you cannot engage with me. Your unmet needs are like a noise which is inhibiting our communication.

How much of the time are you aware of conversation noise? Well, it happens all the time. As you are listening to me, you are probably having a quiet conversation about what I am saying, or about me, or both.

And I could go on telling you in 10 different ways just how much I know about such and such a subject - I could tell you about my degrees in it - I could tell you how I devoted my life to it - I could tell that the Queen of England gave me a knighthood for my services to this subject...

But if you are still having the conversation in your head "What's this got to do with me?", your needs are not being met - and communication is not happening. There is only noise.

Many business leaders I have worked with can't get this. They assume that because they've got to the end of their message, and most of their audience are still in the room with them, and most of them seem to be nodding politely, that their communication has succeeded.

Speaking and talking are happening, undeniably, but not communication. It might be credible, smart, fact-based speaking - but it's not communication. Because the audience has not yet co-created it with them *as* communication.

It's like I am trying to act Gulliver on stage, but you have not yet agreed to make me Gulliver with me.

Or it's likely when I say to Alex, my teenage son, 'So Alex, you're doing your homework now and not playing video games?' and he says 'Yes, Dad!' that I assume homework will occur.

Have you ever been on the receiving end of such a conversation - where someone was talking at you and this had little relevance for you? Were you engaged in the communication? How keen were you to act on what you were told? Not at all.

And that's why I say 'Communication is an act of service.' Because you are serving your audience when you start from the place of Who? Not What or How, or even Why?

The single most transformational question in Unconditional Communication: 'Who is your audience and what do *they* need?

When you begin your communication by selflessly tuning into what is important for your audience, you will greatly increase the likelihood they'll care about what you have to say enough to act on it.

The Nightmare of Believing Content Is King

Have you ever wondered why some people have lots and lots of stuff to say - why they say so much without ever getting to the point? In my corporate work, I ask my groups 'Who's experienced the most amount of slides used in a presentation?"

It's because the instinctual, default way of thinking about communication is 'What shall I say and how shall I say it?' And hidden behind that idea is another idea: The more content the better. The more I say the smarter I'll sound. Or if I just start talking, eventually, surely, I'll say something worthwhile.

The illusion of separation causes anxiety. Too often, we try to fix that anxiety by talking. A lot.

The subtext for this can go even further. One can be: 'I am smarter than my audience (or at least, know more about this topic than they do). So to demonstrate my mastery of the topic, I'll try to cram as much of my knowledge into their heads as I can. They'll feel better for that.'

Another can be: 'I am in fact deeply insecure. So to compensate for my insecurity, I'll just keep talking nonstop. That way I'll never have to hear if I'm actually being relevant or useful.'

Imagine: this evening you are going to a restaurant because you heard the steak is really good there. You are looking forward to that great steak.

But when you get there, the waiter brings you soup. He says, 'This is Gazpacho soup is made from the finest ingredients flown in every morning from the verdant hillsides of Italy! Enjoy!'

You say, 'Can I have the steak?'

The waiter says 'Well, yes, but try the Gazpacho: it's amazing.'

You look a bit askance. But being polite, you consume the Gazpacho,

So later the chef comes out with another bowl of Gazpacho and she says 'I studied for 10 years at the foremost Gazpacho Soup School in the World. My Gazpacho soup gained three Michelin stars! Enjoy'

But you wanted - you have a need for - the steak. And sitting through the Gazpacho is not what you came for. You don't even like Gazpacho!

You can never get enough of what you don't need.

Communication can be a bit like that unless we consider first the needs of our audience. We are in danger of filling them full of our wonderful Gazpacho when what they really need is a steak.

Unless you can anticipate and satisfy the needs of your audience - silence their conversational noise - you will never be creating communication.

Don't start with What do I want to communicate? Or How do I want to communicate it? Or even from Why do I want to communicate it? All great questions, but not at first.

The primary conversation is 'Who is this audience, and what do they need?'

How can I serve my audience?

The third energy which propels the upward spiral of Unconditional Communication is:

CREATED OUTCOMES

Flight: UA 2030. Aircraft: Boeing 737-900. Rows: 20-21.

The Exit rows. I'm sure you've been there. Nice to sit there, because, for the same price, you get an extra six inches of foot space.

First, they come by, when they know rows 20-21 are as full as they are going to get on this flight, about 10 minutes before take off.

Now they remind us that there is an extra cost to sitting in these rows. Not a cost measured in dollars and cents, but in responsibility and integrity.

They say 'Good morning, everybody in rows 20-21, can I have your attention? I need to draw your attention to the fact that you are sitting in the Exit rows of this plane. I would ask that you take out the Safety Card in the pocket of the seat in front of you, and familiarize yourself with its contents.'

And then they say, like The Terminator, 'I'll be back!'

'I'll be back in a few moments to take you through your obligations. Thank you.'

They say this to underline that this is not just a reading exercise.

When they return, they take us through the main highlights of the Safety Card. And then they ask a powerful question:

'Are you willing and able to help in the ways described in the case of emergency?'

This is known as the request for conditionality: do we understand the nature of the promise we are about to make?

The conditions are threefold:

1.   The response to the request is going to be activated in case of emergency. We won't be doing it for show, or to kill time during a long flight.

2.   The response to the request is going to require willingness. You have to be happy to give your service freely.

3.   And the response to the request is going to require ability. You have to be physically capable of executing the actions described on the Safety Card.

Your willingness alone is not sufficient. You can be keen as mustard to help, but if you are sitting there with a broken arm or in recovery from a slipped disc, you really shouldn't be part of this deal. And we can find you a new seat.

Or you can be strong as an ox, but if you are likely to be reduced to a quivering jelly in a real case of emergency, or if you have dark suicidal tendencies and you actually don't mind too much if the plane goes down, then you really shouldn't be part of this deal. And we can find you a new seat.

And then they make another powerful statement: 'I need a verbal yes.'

And they go along each row, one seat at a time, and they engage you in eye contact (they will pause, if your attention is on your iPad, until you look up), and if need be they will point at you. And they will make you say 'Yes.'[7]

Because the designers of this conversation know that public promises are much more likely to be maintained than the private ones inside our heads.

This is an example of pure Unconditional Communication: a clear request met with a clear promise.

When you get married - whether it is in a registry office or in a church - you will be part of a similar Unconditional Communication.

The conditions are there, but they are presented up front, and are non-negotiable. In sickness *and* in health, for example.

And there is a clear request: 'Will you take this man...?' and 'Will you take this woman...?'

---

7. No is an option. There are other seats.

The answer is either Yes or No.

The answer is not going to be 'Maybe.'

Or 'I'll see.'

Or 'Why don't we give it a couple of months as a trial run and see how it goes, and then you can get back to me?'

So there are conditions in Unconditional Communication - it's just that they tend to come before the promise rather than as a bargaining device after it.

And this is how Unconditional Communication makes things happen. Adults freely saying Yes or No. Adults standing in their integrity. Adults being their word.

I think we've become sloppy as a society when it comes to this way of speaking promises. Not only have we lost the capacity to declare Big Promises and commitments and visions (see the next chapter). We've also lost the ability to say Yes or No, and mean it.

This is a society that values the Language of Description. Look at any discussion thread on any news website, or sports website, and you'll see people who think it the best of their communication to describe their opinions, their points of view, their justifications and arguments, the reasons why they are complaining...

You'll hear the Language of Description when you hear someone giving their excuses for not committing, or letting you down. That's when they find their hidden actor: they make their excuses sound so compelling!

The alternative - the Language of Creation: promises, requests, invitations, declarations? Not so present in our society.

You know when you watch the Sunday morning political programs? And there's the latest politician of a note trying to control the conversation? And the interviewer starts his next question with

"I'm looking for a one word answer here.."

You just know what's coming. What's coming is conditional communication. And the condition the politician has is, in effect:

"If I just ignore what you just asked me in terms of 'one word,' and instead I go back to repeat my previous answer in a slightly different form of words, will you let me off the hook and we can mark this down as not so much of a failure in terms of my integrity? Would that be OK?"

And we, the watching audience, say "Yeah, sure, whatever."

Blah, blah, blah.

The world being run at the level of the most immature stage of teenage development.

So, we'll be waiting a long time if we want that reality to change. Politicians will continue to fudge the truth and deflect from the question actually being asked. It's what they are trained for. But you, in your life, today? Maybe there'll be not so long a wait for the Language of Creation to be more a part of your life than the Language of Description.

Make a promise. And stick to it.

If circumstances change so that you can't now maintain your promise, communicate early (before the deadline); explain briefly why, and then negotiate a new promise. And then stick to it.

If you completely screw up a promise and fail to deliver, apologize. Say sorry. But then - and here's the powerful piece of a real apology: ask what discomfort you might have caused the other by failing in your promise. Ratty is likely to minimize for you the impact of your broken promise, but it might be different in the other person's world. So ask.

And then ask what new promise would make that right. And then stick to it.

Unconditional Communication is passionate about making new futures happen, and the building blocks of that creation are requests and promises. Made by adults, not teenagers.

A Wedding. June 12, 2014

Keri and I were guests at the wedding on Thursday afternoon of our friend Elisa and her partner Jeremy, in a glorious outdoor setting in a valley near Masonville, CO. It was a moving event – as all weddings are – and it was inspirational in a way I did not expect it to be.

There were a couple of elements that I was listening for in particular. In my workshops on leadership and language, I use the wedding ritual as an example of an intentional conversation. The world of 'being married' is one created in and through language. Put aside for a few moments all those wonderful feelings and passions of love; unless we can get this thing said, we ain't married at all! So there has to be a question and a response, there has to be an exchange of commitments ('Will you..?'), and another of promises ('I do') – and all wrapped up with a declaration ('I now pronounce you man and wife'). NOW we are married!

And all of that done in public, of course. There has to be at least one witness to any wedding. Whoever designed the first marriage ceremony knew a thing or two about declaring goals in public.

I always love hearing language creating a reality that was not there before the speaking.

The other element I love about the ritual is that both parties get to describe the future, so that both parties are really clear what the agreement is that they are making. ("So, it's about in sickness AND in health? Oh, I thought I could just have you healthy.").

[In consulting, this is known as 'the contracting conversation' – it's essentially the same thing. It's an exchange of requests and promises.]

What was true about this particular ceremony was that the bride and groom had written their own vows (lovely word, 'vow', yes? We don't use it enough...).

Now my Dad, Alan, a very traditionalist Church of England man, was turning in his grave at this point, because he could never see the value of 'these modern fancies'. He liked to play by the rules. But I have grown to love the self-written vow. The Prayer Book language is very, very powerful, but, in the end, it's someone else's script, and a bit of Improv never hurt anyone. We can be the authors of our own lives. And what was undeniably true was that Elisa and Jeremy had poured their hearts into their vows, had found the words to name the appreciation and wonder they had for each other, to such an extent that Jeremy was crying before he even started his, and Elisa had to hand her vows, on a piece of paper, to the Minister before she had finished hers, so he could read them on her behalf.

So all of that was wonderful, and what I was looking forward to. But just in case I was persuading myself that all of this was being done for my entertainment, Great Spirit had a couple of surprises in store for me.

Almost the first thing the Minister said was 'We are here today to celebrate Love. And as Scripture reminds us, Love is the nearest experience we have to Being God on this Earth.'

And at this moment, I kid you not, a cloud shifted and sunlight bathed the whole congregation and the wedding party. What theater! God, of course, hails from Colorado, but that was a special moment from the Big Guy!

But there were two other moments that moved me the most.

One of those moments was this. Before the exchange of vows, the Minister looked into each of their faces in turn and said:

'Jeremy. You are a builder. You build things. You create beautiful homes out of basic materials. You help your clients' dreams become a reality. You have vision. You also know the sweat and hard work required to raise a house out of the ground. ALL of these qualities that you use in your work, you will need to build this marriage.

And Elisa. You are a waitress and barmaid. That means you serve. You know the beauty of service. You know how to anticipate a need and deliver on it. You know how to put stressed and tired customers at ease so they can enjoy their night out. You know how to put a smile on your own face for the good of others, even on those days when you think you can't find a smile inside you at all. ALL of these qualities that you use in your work, you will need to serve the health of this marriage.'

A relationship, then, is work, and the work is Love.

And finally, one other piece of wisdom from the Minister (who, by the way, didn't look a day over 30). He came to the exchange of the rings. And he told a story that before the ceremony, in the planning stages, he'd had a conversation with Jeremy in which Jeremy had said that he and Elisa 'weren't going to do rings; we are going to get tattoo rings instead!'

'This' said the Minister, with a heavy sigh that belied his years 'is a common thought in these days...'

But the Minister had persuaded them otherwise, and for one critical reason: that the tattoo is permanent, but wearing the ring is a choice. 'You may never, in fact, take off your wedding ring. But every day you have it on is a reminder to you of the choice you are making to be in this marriage. 'A marriage' he said 'doesn't stick to you. You stick to it.'

As the writer Peter Block says 'Without our ability to say No, our Yes means nothing.'

Keri and I had to leave soon after the ceremony – our eldest son Oliver had turned 18 that same day, so we were on our way to celebrate that milestone too – but already there was music, and there was going to be singing, and dancing, and eating together, and storytelling, because that's what people like to do when they are really happy, and as we drove back down the valley, the sun was still shining.

ENTR'ACTE:
LOVE AND FEAR

Our only failure is not to love

Father Richard Rohr

We can't go much further in our journey into communication without you and me talking about love. I would like to suggest that love is an idea whose time has come. Who'd have thought it?

When I was studying literature, I was studying love, because art is created through the creative energy of love, because love wants to express itself and make a difference through its expression.

When I was performing theater, I was performing love, because theater is the work of bringing the formless into form. And you do that so others can see, experience feel something meaningful to them.

When I was teaching presentation skills in the business world in the 1990s, I was teaching love. I never told my clients that, because, as my first mentor Peter Sole taught me 'There is no point in scaring the horses.' But I was teaching love. Because there is no point in presenting anything to anyone unless you love who you are as the presenter: that you can believe 'I have something to say.' And there is no point in presenting unless you can love what you want to present, and love why you are presenting it - what it will do for others. It was this perspective - rather than giving my clients communication tips and techniques - that would truly deliver them from their fear of presenting.

Love is a formless abstraction unless expressed in action.

When I say love, I know that you know that I don't mean romantic, interpersonal love. That would be creepy. Besides, I know how many bad experiences we've all had in the realm of interpersonal love. I hear that your parents didn't love you enough. That your spouse didn't show you enough respect. I know that 'love' in that form has had many disappointments.

But I mean the love that binds and drives the universe.

I mean love as the ultimate grounding in which we all exist and from which we all create. And that flows through us trying to find its expression in our action. That love does not turn itself off when we have done our Sunday morning duty by going to church. It is trying to come through us, whether we are a builder or a barmaid, whether we are author or a doctor, whether we are a plumber or a politician or a CEO.

And in that love we are truly connected, because we all share the same source.

The force that grows my fingernails grows yours too. Life, wanting to be more of itself. Love, wanting to experience itself more. Through you.

The Hindu language has a word of greeting: Namaste. It means: 'I bow to the divine in you.'

It says 'I see you in me. I see that you and me are the same. Made in the same image, from formless into form, and as loving creators.'

I don't know of a single business problem, manifested in the need for a difficult conversation, which would not be better started with the words 'I love you.' Not 'I love you' because I'm attracted to you physically. But 'I love you' because 'Namaste': I and you are from the same source.

Your Ratty is screaming at you right now as you read this. But Ratty is a deceiver. Ratty is making the very world you are frustrated by.

Performance Appraisals? Don't you know how much everyone hates those? Throw the whole damned form away and replace it with this opening to the conversation:

> Hello [name].
>
> I love you.
>
> What do you want?
>
> How can I help?

Love is the emotion of merging, of becoming One. Love is a way of pushing through into the One. We treat love and hate and the other emotions like they are all on the same level, but they're not. Hate, fear, lust, greed, jealousy – all that comes from the ego. Only love comes from the soul. When you identify with your soul, you live in a loving universe. The soul loves everybody. It's like the sun. It brings out the beauty in each of us.

Ram Dass

There's another reason that love matters so much to our collective futures.

The word love comes from an Old English word 'lief.' It means gladly or willingly. It means, I don't mind. We could go as *lief* North or South. It's up to you. I'll follow you in any case.

The old word *lief* underlines that the most powerful expression of love is to love someone as they are, not as we'd want them to be. Unconditionally. I'll love you no matter what happens. I don't need you to change, and certainly not to change for my expectations or demands.

That's our job, then. To love unconditionally. That's when we are at our most loving.

This form of love - *lief* - is most urgent today in a world where we have been encouraged to be dismissive, judgemental and angry with others.

Instead of loving, we have allowed ourselves to be governed by the universal paradigm for humankind: *we are disappointed with others, and want them to be different.*

God Loves Ariel

Ariel, my client from Mexico, books a one to one session with me. He heard me say that any audience he will ever speak to as a leader is on his side. He heard me say that any audience he will ever speak to as a leader wants him to succeed. He's struggling with this.

He tells me that he is Catholic, and every Sunday, in church back home in Mexico City, his priest preaches from the pulpit that God is Love, and that everyone is born from Love, and He sent his son Jesus Christ to remind everyone that they are always, in all ways, whatever their faults and sins, loved.

And Ariel tells me that he sits there hearing this and thinking: 'Even me? Surely God wouldn't say that if he knew me and my life. These other people around me, surely yes. But me?'

Ariel tells me that hearing me say 'Every audience is on your side' is like him hearing 'God loves Ariel.' He accepts that other people might have kind audiences, but from where he stands, his audiences look like they are trying to catch him out.

The fact is God loves Ariel whether Ariel can believe that or not. Indeed his doubt is what is preventing him from having a fuller relationship with his God.

And we, apparently, would prefer to be right that audiences are separate from us and adversarial to us, than to experience what is possible when we let go of that belief.

Audiences want you to be good? 'Even me?'

That 'Your audience is on your side' is true whether you believe that or not, and it has amazed me how rigorously people hold onto their belief that their audience is out to get them.

It is that belief that prevents them from having a fuller and richer and more authentic connection to their audience.

As proof, I ask Ariel how many times he has sat in an audience and willed the speaker to fail. To be bad. To be humiliated. Maybe once. Maybe on Ariel's worst day, on the morning of his worst hangover, after an argument with his wife, and when he's just found out that the quarterly results were dire - maybe on that one day, he'd wanted the speaker to be bad, because that day he wanted the whole world to burn. But the other 99.99% of the time? Not at all.

But *my* God can't love me, and *my* audience is not on my side.

So people believe that the audience is out to get them, and it's inevitable they'll find that.

Your audience will pick up on your inner stance that you believe yourself to be in an adversarial relationship to them, and will get freaked out by it. They may not be conscious of that, but they will, sooner or later, begin to respond accordingly. They'll begin to wonder what's wrong - why this isn't a natural and relaxed engagement. They'll begin to look for the reasons for what's wrong - and, humans being humans, they won't start with themselves: they'll blame you for it. So the very thing you were scared of - that the audience is out to get you - is being made manifest, and the source of that manifestation is your own belief.

As if it is ever any other way.

Communication becomes transformational when we serve the needs of our audience before caring about getting our own needs met.

And, here's the kicker, what is also true is that we create our audience.

I look at my audience and I see tricksters and villains. Or I look at my audience and see people waiting patiently to have their needs met. And that's all happening 'in here' and not 'out there.'

Separation is frightening. So, why would we feel the need to scare ourselves so badly?

Fear

The opposite of Love is not hate but Fear.

How do you think Love is doing in this world right now? In your life?

Is there more Love, or more Fear?

If more Fear, what is it that we are afraid of?

I would suggest that the Illusion of Separation is the source of our Fear; and our Fear is the cause of our Separation.

Our separation has been solidified in our mental models of what communication is.

If I were to ask you to draw a depiction of two people communicating, you would most probably draw two stick figures, separated by a gap. And maybe some speech bubbles trying to cross that gap.

And this is the start of our difficulties with communication. The more we start from a place of being separate, the more distant we make ourselves, the more we insist there is a gap when in fact we are already connected, the more differences will actually arise.

Separation causes comparison.

Comparison causes competition.

Competition breeds scarcity.

Scarcity causes anxiety.

Anxiety grows into Fear.

And Fear, when asked to say why it's present, says 'Because of them, over there!'

We need to kill Them. I don't mean them, over there, but the concept of Them at all. The very notion of Them as other human beings who are separate from, and dangerous to, our well-being.

Because that Them is always going to turn out to be just like us.

I'm in a client firm running a story circle exercise.

Fifteen leaders sitting on chairs arranged in a circle. They are sharing the homework: come prepared to tell us a three minute story of something that happened to you in the past that has helped shape who you are in the present.

Fifteen leaders from 10 different countries, so there are different details and situations and certainly different cultures mentioned.

But the stories have very similar themes. A difficult situation left behind. A problem overcome. A challenge learned from. A mistake made that turned into inspiration (once they'd got past the shame of the mistake). Love lost. Love won.

Because these are the essential drumbeats of human life. We want things to go one way, but then circumstances cause that expectation to be disappointed. And then we pick ourselves up again, and carry on, and we grow.

Russian, Chinese, Turkish, French: all the same struggles. And every time a story is told, there is the same response from the audience:

'I get that. I get you. I see me in you!'

I recognize your world in my world.

You are just like me.

I see you in me.

Every single time I run these story circles.

It's all one.

There is no Them there.

Now if I hear the sound of the genuine in me, and if you hear the sound of the genuine in you, it is possible for me to go down in me and come up in you. So that when I look at myself through your eyes having made that pilgrimage, I see in me what you see in me and the wall that separates and divides will disappear and we will become one, because the sound of the genuine makes the same music.

Howard Thurman, "The Sound of the Genuine," Baccalaureate Address, Spelman College (May 4, 1980)

One of the things these 15 leaders got was that sharing their story, telling the truth, being real about their mistakes and weaknesses, in fact made them stronger, not weaker. Because, being human, their audiences had also experienced similar mistakes and weaknesses themselves. So hearing the speaker's mistakes made it more likely to accept their own. Communication as an act of service.

There was once a guy in my workshop who had trained to be an astronaut. Never, before or since, have I met an astronaut. His 'form' - his training - was different to mine. But what he wanted to share - his struggles with failure and fear - was universal and *just like me*.

My workshop participants found that their vulnerability made them more real and more connected to the whole, rather than what their Ratty might have tried to predict for them: 'If I show myself in all my flaws, I will be in danger of being cast out.'

When we get to see that we are all, in fact, the same - and not Us and Them - now we can build something powerful together. We've no need to be distracted by background agendae or hidden motivations and fears.

If you are holding back then you can't find out what you, or others, are capable of.

Little Victories or Bigger Callings?

I'm in Beirut, about to launch a leadership program for a company there.

The client sends a car to pick me up from the hotel, and the driver navigates us toward the venue through the rush hour traffic.

Avoiding the jammed highway, he turns down a small side street, with cars parked solidly along one side of the road. There is not much room to maneuver, but it doesn't cause our driver to slow down any.

About half way hurtling down this narrow street, a homeowner, appearing seemingly out of nowhere, steps out from between two parked cars and into our path. I don't know if my driver is to blame for going too fast, or the neighbor is to blame for not looking before stepping out. Both, I'm sure. We speed past, and the neighbor leaps backward out of our way.

I turn around and look out the back window of our car to see if the guy is OK. I see him straighten up, turn to us, as we accelerate away from him, and watch him, with grand intentionality, giving us the Beirut equivalent of the middle finger.

I turn back around to talk to the driver, but before I can speak, I see him look at the homeowner in his rear view mirror, and return the same middle finger gesture.

One hour later, I tell this story at the start of the leadership program. I say something about this program being an invitation to rise above that sort of tit-for-tat small mindedness, and reach for something bigger.

Two days later, at the end of the program, I give the participants time to reflect on their learnings, and set themselves a Big Why for being a leader in the world.

Participants stand up, one after another, and give two or three minute statements of their best intentions.

The last participant up said just one thing, with reference to my story:

'I lead, because there has to be more to life than chasing little victories.'

How true: there is so much more. And that's what the next part of this book is about.

PART THREE

YOUR JOURNEY MATTERS TO EVERYONE

Let me tell you about the four conversations.

The first conversation is the foundational one. It is the conversation beyond language, where we experience ourselves intimately connected to all of reality within and around us. It's the grounding of silence and peace out of which all the other conversations arise. Eckhart Tolle famously called it 'The Now', and many other spiritual teachers have named it Unconditioned Awareness or The Peace Which Passeth All Understanding.

My wife Keri accesses that space when she works in the garden; she disappears into the zone of nature.

It's where you are trying to get to when you meditate.

It's where the yoga teachers take us at the end of the vishana flow, in the corpse pose, flat on our backs and unmoving, fully awake and yet completely relaxed. Symbolically letting go of all our temporary and human-made worries and concerns, and yielding into the sacred space where we realize none of that other stuff truly matters.

Why do we all have that serene smile on our face at the end of our yoga practice? It's because we've just come Home.

So that is the first conversation.

Then, second, there is the conversation with our self - the internal dialogue, the incessant chatter of mind, the voice that is seeking to guide us and explain the world to us. Ratty or Angelo? That's why the serene smile caused by the first conversation usually only lasts as long as reaching the exit door of the yoga studio: it's because Ratty has reminded us that we have stuff to get on with. 'Stop being so serene: it's time to get busy!'

Much of that stuff we have to do is done with and through others. This leads to the third conversation - the external dialogue where we share our thoughts with others through spoken and written language, and share our presence through our body language and facial expressions. The third conversation is the one we most think about when we hear the word 'communication.' But can you see how that third conversation is likely informed by the quality of the first two?

And then there is a fourth conversation, although we rarely give ourselves the chance to participate in it. The fourth conversation is the conversation our life is having with us. I invite you to understand that your life is trying to tell you something.

Joseph Campbell was an American mythologist, writer and lecturer who worked out through his studies that all myths, all stories have the same deep structure. Whether he was studying Chinese, African, Hindu, Aborigine or Greek mythology, they all followed a similar shape or structure. He called it the Monomyth. And it became more popularly known as The Hero's Journey.

Why do all those myths have the same flow, the same elements in roughly the same order? Is it because all the ancient myth-makers went to the same screenwriting school? Hardly.

It's because life itself has that structure.

Life, and stories, hold to the deep structure of beginning, middle and end.

In the Hero's Journey, there are three stages laid on top of that: Separation, Initiation and Return.

The hero[8] is called on an adventure, which means she needs to leave - be separated from - her familiar world and enter a new,

---

8. Much as Hero has come, over the years, to be attached to masculine warrior archetypes, the word originally simply meant 'the main character of a story.' And that, in your life, is always going to be you, whatever gender you identify as. You are always the hero, whatever you are up to. Joseph Campbell also said: "A hero is someone who has given his or her life to something bigger than oneself." And that, I hope, is also you.

unfamiliar world. The separation - the Call to Adventure - is the motive force, the catalyst for change.

Simply because that new world of adventure is unfamiliar, it is going to throw up challenges to overcome. The hero is going to be initiated - trained, in simple terms - in new skills or qualities. There will be dangers, and there will he helpers along the way. There will be moments of blazing certainty and optimism, and there will also be moments of existential doubt ('I can't go on.'). Campbell called this The Belly of the Whale, referencing Jonah in the Bible story, when all appeared to be lost.

But that's not the end of the journey. There is still forward movement. The goal will be achieved - the gold recovered; the princess rescued; the dragon slain - but the story is not over even then, even at that high point of outer success.

Because finally there will be some movement back home - the Return. The question for the Hero now is: 'What have I learned, and how can I share that learning with my tribe back home - if they ever have to go on their own journeys?' Campbell called this The Treasure. Not the gold, the thing of form that the heroes thought they were questing for: but the formless, timeless wisdom that can help them, and others in the future, to suffer less and be happy more.

Dorothy in the Wizard of Oz does not stay in Oz, but is transported home. But it is not the place she left. Why? It's because of the experiences she had on her journey: she now does not see that same old place in the same old way. She brings to an old place a new sense of perspective. She meets the same old friends and family as before - but the way she sees them has changed, profoundly. At the beginning of The Wizard of Oz, she leaves a place she is frustrated and bored by, and returns to it as a place she never wants to leave again, because she now sees there is so much love in it.

In this sense, then, there is no 'going home,' because you will be different when you get there.

And that's why, despite the fact that The Hero's Journey is drawn as a circle on the page, it is never, in fact, a circle. It is an upward spiral.

What stops your life being a set of circles - 'Here I am again!' - is your willingness to be courageous, face your initiation, grow from it, and, above all, learn.

And that doesn't just matter to you. It matters for others in your life.

When you share what you have learned, you will inspire and move others to rise up their own spiral.

The more you live your life as someone committed to moving through the upward spiral, the more you will inspire others to live their lives like that too.

No life is ever pointless or without meaning (although depression, for example, is a curse that makes some people think that).

Whatever your journey is, whether it be to slay a magical dragon in a dangerous cave in Erebor, or whether it be to parent a child through their doubts and insecurities in South London, your life can always be a Treasure for others.

Calling on the Universe

Dorothy doesn't have a choice about her journey. She is swept up in a real (and then metaphorical) tornado.

We get to activate our own Hero's Journeys by declaring what is known as the Call to Adventure.

That Call you make may be activated by restlessness, or boredom. Or it may be propelled by some seemingly external cause such as a serious illness or financial catastrophe. In the Hero's Journey cycle, Campbell calls it The Wasteland. It's the place that used to be your normal and known safe place, but now it's profoundly changed, and you can't, or won't, remain there.

One way or another, the Call sounds like: 'Enough! There has to be more than this!'

Your saying 'This is what matters to me' is a Call that then activates the universe.

And then what happens - always - is that you get tested. The universe responds to your call and says 'Are you sure?'

James Bond is sipping champagne on a deserted beach with his unbelievably beautiful lover. But then his phone rings.

He takes the Call from M and says 'Yes, of course I will go and kill the villain in his secret lair.'

And the universe - in the form of the villain's henchmen and Bond's own personal peccadillos and values - responds by saying 'Are you sure you will succeed, Mr Bond?'

The Journey does not go directly from Bond's acceptance of the mission to him killing the villain. He has to be tested. He has to apply the resources he has acquired from other journeys, from other cases and stories.

This is what actually happens. First he has to get on a plane and be almost pushed out of it and then he has to find a car and then be almost driven off the road by henchmen in other cars and then he has to have a big fight with three other henchmen and a dangerous hat and then he has to be distracted by a beautiful woman and make passionate love to her, only to be attacked by other henchmen who have been hiding under the bed, and then he has to play a long game of cards with a cheating associate of the villain and then he has to escape some sharks... And only then does he finally get to kill the villain.

The challenges are what make the movie interesting. The almost-failing is marbled into the drama.

It's what we, the audience, are paying for in the movie house.

And it is what we, as our own heroes in our own dramas, are actually here for. We'd prefer a life without drama and setbacks. But how's that wish working for you?

In the movie, we want the dramas to keep coming, because it's entertaining to watch them happen to someone else.

In our lives, we believe we want the dramas to stop (unless we are addicted to life drama, which is another pathology, like depression). But we don't get to stop the dramas happening to us, except by facing them, dealing with them, and learning from them.

The journey you are really on is the one you are struggling with right now.

What are the resources you have acquired and can express in the furtherance of your quest? And what new resources do you need to develop?

That is the conversation life is trying to have with you.

My client, Mark, wants to take his leadership to the next level. That's his declaration.

And then there is a major shift in the marketplace that suddenly threatens the well-being of his business and everyone employed in it.

The universe is saying to my client 'Are you sure about that leadership thing? Are you sure you are big enough for your declaration? How are you going to respond if we throw doubt and the potential for utter failure in your path?"

My client spirals down into self-pity. He's blaming himself, he's doubting himself, he thinks life is being unfair. He sees the future as dark and unwelcoming.

He is in the belly of the whale.

And later that same day (April 15th, 2019) a cathedral burns in Paris and within 24 hours a billion dollars has been pledged because human beings have a deep instinct to face into tragedy and rebuild from the ashes.

The universe then says to my client 'Are you sure about that self-pity thing? Are you really going to give in to self-doubt and despair? Are you sure *you* can't rebuild your business like this ancient cathedral will surely rebuild?'

And so he responds. He decides to give 18 more hours to wallowing in self-pity, and then he girds his loins and shows up like a Hero rather than a Victim. Someone committed to something bigger than his fears.

The journey you are really on is the one you are struggling with right now. Life loves that you have set goals and visions. That's part of the game. But life is really interested in how you respond to the struggle.

That's the conversation life is wanting to have with you.

'Are you sure?'

'Wherever you are right now, are you sure there isn't more?'

'Are you sure there isn't more for you, and in you?'

Being present to the fourth conversation is what turns your life into an upward spiral rather than a repeating circle.

Facing into the lessons - rather than distracting yourself by solving immediate, relatively simple and surface-level problems - is where the growth is.

That's an unconditional relationship to life.

Conditional says 'I must try to minimize failure and disappointment. A good life is one where only good things happen to me.'

Unconditional says 'Everything is happening for a purpose that I can declare at any moment as significant, and can learn from.'

Conditional says 'Manage my life. Get through it as best I can."

Unconditional says 'Bring it on! I will embrace it all, apparently good and apparently bad.'

I have a friend whose fiance is always complaining about his bosses: 'Why do I always seem to work for jerks? He is on a quest to be a great employee and do great work, but he keeps on being disappointed by his bosses. So he keeps quitting - or getting let go - and starts on his quest again. He's trapped in a circle, and it will only become a spiral when he works out his contribution to the problem he's complaining about.

Wherever you go, there you are. If there are patterns like this in our lives, we have to look at our part in making them happen. We're not experiencing our life, we're co-creating it. Life isn't happening to us, but through us.

The more awake you are - the more present you are to your life and the patterns and the forces at play within it - the more intentional your life will become. And the more valuable you will be to others, because you'll be able to share your story and realizations with others.

That's why you matter so much. We couldn't do this thing called life without you.

My friend Ronnie is at a career crossroads. He's had a massively successful career already. He is faced with many options, and could pretty much have his pick of the next, best job.

'What shall I do next?' he asks.

I say, 'The question is not what you should do next; the question is what are you here for?'

Vocation

Today.. "Let your life speak" means something else to me: "Before you tell your life what you intend to do with it, listen to what it intends to do with you. Before you tell your life what truths and values you have decided to live up to, let your life tell you what truths you embody, what values you represent."

In other words, your life is not about you. You are about a larger thing called Life. You are not your own. You are an instance of a universal and eternal pattern. Life is living itself in you. The myriad forms of life in the universe are merely parts of the One Life—that many of us call "God." You and I don't have to figure it all out, fix everything, or do life perfectly by ourselves. All we have to do is participate in this One Life. To find our unique niche in that Always Larger Life is what we mean by "vocation."

Parker Palmer, Quaker teacher and activist

In search of Bigger Futures, more of us, I think, need to engage with this fourth conversation. We need to start making more commitments than complaints. We need to start making some big declarations of purpose and power. We need to hear ourselves saying something that really matters, and that could move the world.

How small our dreams have become...a steady career; a certain amount of wealth; being, most of the time, a fairly good parent or spouse. Wonderful as those things are, is this really why we are here?

How sad that our identities have become reduced to being happy consumers and not powerful creators.

For Bigger Futures, more of us need to show up with something to say.

What's Your Big Idea?

A few years back I was invited to do a TEDx talk.

Given my profession, writing and delivering the talk was not going to be a challenge for me.

It was the meta level of what was happening that I loved. That someone would come to me and say:

"David, I know you could probably say a heck of a lot about a heck of a lot of subjects - but if you were forced to choose one idea, to speak about it for 18 minutes, and you genuinely felt that this idea was one worth spreading for the greater good of all humanity...

...What would you say?"

What does it take to really have something to say? What does it mean to be a stand for something?

In the TED brand, being a stand literally means standing in the red circle, in the spotlight, in front of the audience - and, of course, the future audience that is going to see the video for years afterward.

It's an experience I would recommend to anyone. One reason is because I believe it will grow you to get clear on what you'd commit to declaring to the world. To say, 'This is why I am here; and this is the idea I am prepared to stand behind!' It's entirely different than being expert in

What's your big idea? What's your bold declaration?

What's the one idea you will be unconditional about?

The second reason I'd recommend this process is that it is like a Call to Adventure. Declare it, and the universe will respond by testing you.

My TEDx talk was about 'being your word,' and never, before or since, have I been given so many opportunities where my own integrity was put to the test. At about this time, I resigned from an extremely lucrative contract with a client because I was appalled by the behaviours at play by some leaders within that project. I wanted no more of that in my life. So I quit. As you can probably imagine, it had immediate consequences for my cashflow, and for my reputation in that firm. I am still experiencing the side effects of that decision now.

I could have stayed silent and taken the money. I could have been what others wanted me to be: a well-behaved consultant, happy to be employed. But the trouble was, I was about to step on a stage and tell people to honour their instincts, and to do what they knew to be right, rather than what was expedient.

From that time on, I have always described that period of my life as 'You do the TED talk, and then the TED talk does you.'

The other dimension to this, of course, is that you choosing to stand up, on any real or metaphorical stage, will provoke the response of those who have chosen to be bystanders and commentators. As Alan and I used to say in our theater days 'In the cheap seats, everyone's a critic.'

If you choose to speak from that place of authenticity and truth, there will be haters. You will be sharing the light, and the darkness doesn't like that. You will be condemned by some. And they have found ways to be really condemning.

So, knowing that's a likely outcome, what would you say in any case?

What word would you stand behind?

How will you be unconditional?

The downsides to showing up in life that way are so much less real than your Ratty would have you believe. Because life is on our side.

We Live in A Kind Universe

In our frustration, we may ask, why can't we just be nicer to each other?

It's because, when we act or speak in an unkind way, we've momentarily forgotten something about the nature of the universe we are in.

We've momentarily allowed ourselves to believe that we live in a brutish, short and hostile universe, where bad things happen for no reason to good people, and where what we are looking for - respect, acknowledgment, help, care, love - is scarce. So scarce, that if we don't get it, someone else will take it. This universe does not have an upward spiral - it is a nasty circle of little victories at the cost of others. So we fight, brutishly, for the scraps.

For those who are unkind and selfish as a default behavior, it's not that they momentarily forgot something about the nature of the universe; perhaps they were never given the opportunity to know it. But you and I don't have that excuse.

The Hero's Journey is a profoundly kind structure, and its ultimate purpose is to remind us that we live in a kind universe. Because it tells us that nothing you are called upon to deal with in your life, however painful, is designed to disable you or make you look bad or find you lacking. All of it, the good, the bad and the crazy, is designed to ask you what you are able to learn from it, and what you are able to create out of it. Because your movie hasn't ended yet.

When we know that the bigger, wider universe that holds our life is for us and not against us, we can relax into our own journey more. We will certainly need to fight the fight when it is the time to do that, because challenge and pain is marbled into life like the fat in a steak. And it won't ever be pleasant to feel that pain. But there is more in us than that pain; and more waiting for us beyond it.

Why I Wept. Sept 27, 2018

I help out at an annual leadership development program for a global company.

We were coming to the close of the second of the three residential workshops which form a significant part of the participants' year long journey - this time held in the beautiful city of Strasbourg.

We were celebrating with a considerable meal of (mainly) meat and wine. As I am not physically involved during the third workshop, this was the last time I would be with many of the 30 young leaders, and, very kindly, they presented me, as the dinner came to a close, with a gift.

YOUR JOURNEY MATTERS TO EVERYONE

A human skull.

Those of you who know my work will understand the significance of this. Those of you who have not yet been part of one of my communication workshops will not. But let me just say that, if ever you have been given a gift that feels like 'Well, that's nice, but not really essential to my life' - like a pair of socks for Christmas, for example - and if you've also ever been given a gift that strikes you to your core in terms of its relevance for you, then this skull falls into the second category.

And so, here we all are in this restaurant in Strasbourg, and, as is the way with this sort of public gift-giving, the cry went up 'Speech, speech, speech!'

And I think the group was surprised by how I responded to their request, particularly since I'd spent much of my time in the workshops teaching them what I believe to be effective communication. It should have been a simple task for me to string a few sentences together in the moment, and tell them how grateful I was for their gift.

Instead, I wept.

I was going to write 'I cried like a baby' - but I think that babies cry to signal that something has gone wrong - feed me, change me, hold me and make me feel less alone!

Adults weep, on the other hand, when they realize that they are involved in something transformational. We weep at death, at grief, at loss, and sometimes, even at joy.

So I wept, and then I took some breaths to recover, like a pro speaker does....and then I wept again.

And I was present enough to look into the faces of some of the group and see them thinking 'Well, this is not what we had in mind!' – but, at last, one the audience - you know who you are! - spoke out and said 'David, you don't really have to say anything, you know.'

And with that I sat down, and, they being kind people, the group applauded and cheered, and we all got on with the remainder of the dinner.

It could have been that this group of 30 leaders in that restaurant in Strasbourg will never know what I was going to say to them that night.

But they will now.

Here's what I wanted to say:

"Thank you for this skull. The character who holds a skull like this in the communication workshop you've done with me is literally faced with death, and the inevitability of his own. He is also faced with a choice about how he responds to that truth. He could tell himself a story about all that is lost, and all that has gone wrong in his life, and how true that all is, and how miserable life is. Or he could ask himself a question: 'Until I become a skull like this in the dead ground, until I die, how shall I live?'

One of the reasons I wept was because I'd been very present to this sort of conversation over the last few weeks. Not just for me. I'm old enough to have had two mid-life crises, and only the first one, aged 39, was founded on my sudden, apparently surprising, realization that I too was not immortal, and would one day die. (The second mid-life crisis is covered well in my interview with Oprah, whenever that happens).

So, no, not just for me. But because I'd been staying, prior to this workshop, with my Mum, who is in the last phase - however long that might be - of her own life. And we had talked over many days about what that meant to her, and what her best memories were, and also how she was deciding to live in the last phase of her own life, before she too becomes - like this gift you have given me - a skull in the dead ground.

So I was weeping partly as a man grieving the anticipated death of his mother.

And I was weeping because your gift had touched me, not like socks, but because I had realized that you had recognized that this gift is resonant to the space we had all created in this leadership journey together: in other words, it mattered.

And people do not act enough toward each other like they matter in this world, I think. And I was weeping because that's a shame.

And I wept because, although it might be a shame that people don't treat each other like they matter enough, that is not inevitable. And that the source of a different, better way is available to us every time we open our mouth, or, even better, when we keep it shut.

You'll probably recall how I talked about being invited to do my own TEDx talk, and how the biggest result of that was not that I now have a few thousand likes on YouTube (Whohoo! Result!!) but because I'd discovered the research that suggests that every one of us is, on average, going to speak 14,000 words today, and tomorrow, and every day until we become the skull. One interpretation I have made of this research is that it explains how this world is so goddamn noisy. Yada, yada, yada, blah, blah, blah.

The other interpretation I have made of this research is that everything you say comes out of that limitless, empty, comforting space we call silence.

And remaining in silence is always an option, and might, I'd invite you to consider, be an option you take at least once out of your next ten utterances. Because human beings are the only creatures on God's Green Earth who can speak, and NONE OF THEM HAVE TO! Honestly, you don't. Even if you were desperate, as an adult, you could cry like a baby tomorrow and eventually, if you cried enough like a baby, you would eventually get fed. Or changed. But you are unlikely to stay silent. You are going to wake up tomorrow and something inside you is going to compel you to try to speak 14,000 words.

Or you could ask a variant of that guy's question prompted by him gazing at the skull: 'Given I will one day die, how do I choose to speak?'

And I wanted to tell you all, in that restaurant in Strasbourg, that this is the question I want to leave you with, and the one that could be transformational for you. Given you could say nothing, what will you choose to say today, with intentionality, and with due consideration (we called it 'rehearsal' in the workshop)?

And where will you come from when you say those considered words? Will you come from a place of fear and anxiety ('I wonder how they'll respond to this; I wonder if they find me out')?

Or will you come from a place of love ('I wouldn't be saying this, however apparently difficult the topic is, unless I was committed to creating something bigger for us all beyond this difficult situation')?

In other words, there is a kindness at the foundation of all this communication work (and that is very different from 'David Firth says you should be more kind!'). The kindness is that you are - really, truly - allowed to speak from what truly matters to you. This is Your Word. It really is.

And the kindness is that, if you work from what would serve your audience rather than what you think would impress them, then bigger outcomes will come from that. The kindness is that if you enter into real conversations with each other, as opposed to planning strategies for influencing, persuading or manipulating people, you'll create a bigger space for collective wisdom and engagement to rise up than you'd ever thought possible on your own.

And all of that is wrapped up in a thing you now know as The Hero's Journey - much misunderstood, by some, as a template for aggressive masculinity - but which is, as far as I am concerned, a universal structure for understanding how life tends to work itself out, and a profoundly kind structure. Because it tells us that nothing you are called upon to deal with in your life, however painful, is designed to disable you or make you look bad or find you lacking. All of it, the good, the bad and the crazy, is designed to ask you what you are able to learn from it, and what you are able to create out of it.

And that is the sort of kindness, I assert, that your own leadership journey needs - and, bigger than that, what the world needs right now."

And that is why I wept.

Now, having said all that: what would it take to go on collective Hero's Journeys? What if we, together, could declare our Calls to Adventure; what if, together, we could experience the initiation and the growth that comes from that?

That's what the final part of this book is about.

PART FOUR

SHAPING OUR WORLD

The Treasure is not the Adventure

This book is based on the essential mutuality or co-creative nature of communication.

My communication does not exist - expect as noise - until it is made into something bigger by you. So my communication has to be an invitation for that - an opening for you to bring whatever you can bring, on our journey together on the upward spiral. It's not about me, it's about us, and what we can create together. Like the improvisors and the audience at The Comedy Store.

In this last part of the book, I want to explore the possibilities for this approach in communal communication (see the repeating stem there in all these words: communication, community, communal: *com-* meaning *together*). Because what we have now in communal communication is desperately thin and unproductive.

I think that one of our greatest challenges as a society is how we hold more effective conversations at the collective level. And by effective, I mean large scale conversations that tap into our collective knowledge, talent and willingness - so that we can activate that as a way of solving some of our biggest collective problems. Because all the biggest problems we face in our society - climate change; racial, sexual and economic discrimination; the education and development of the younger generations for a world that exists now rather than what was relevant in the past - all of these are collective problems. No great leader is going to solve these challenges on our behalf. No one is coming.

We have to move from *I/You* to *We*.

We have to move from the idea that 'public discourse' is all about how our leaders sound when they are speaking to us (e.g. their tone of voice and sense of respect) to something much more constructive and transformational than that. Something bigger. Public discourse that causes change to happen, together.

What I am pointing to is the capacity to hold large scale conversations that matter. These conversations will matter because they reach down to the problems beneath the (apparent) problem, and by so doing will invite collective wisdom, experience and commitment in their solution. As citizens, we will not be invited to merely be good audiences for others' messages, but active participants in our created future.

The Culture Made Me Do It: bringing about a collective identity shift and an end to the consumer society

Here is the shape of the world[9].

It's a triangle.

A hierarchy pointing upward to the top.

For all our recent flattening of societies and organizations - stripping away the old layers of middle management, for example, to become leaner - the human mind still tends to work in terms of hierarchy. There is someone up there with more power and control than us down here.

When these same organizations and institutions choose to gather their constituents together, they turn that same triangle on its axis.

So rather than causing us to gaze upward, the shape of the gathering persuades us all to look to the front of the room. There's usually a stage there. The stage is usually raised, to subtly reinforce status. On the stage is either a small group of leaders, sitting behind a table. Or a single person: the CEO, or the Candidate, or the hired motivational speaker.

Our job as participants is usually to sit in rows, looking out front toward the source of power or influence on the stage, and at the back of our colleagues' heads. And maybe our only

---

9. With thanks to Peter Block for showing me this.

real participation will be to fill out the feedback forms at the end of the event.

We've constructed events like this because our leaders have feared the collective.

When my clients consider bringing their employees together for a large scale event - a conference or a company offsite, for example - their minds immediately go to how they will control the crowd.

They think it's going to be chaos unless they impose their control. As a result, most larger gatherings are micromanaged experiments in eliminating surprise. Every minute of the conference is planned on a spreadsheet, even the breaks. Even if there are 'breakout sessions' - because leaders have woken up to their idea that there should be some sort of interactivity - that very interaction is controlled. In our breakouts, we participants are told what to speak about, and with whom, and told when to be back - so we can all keep the larger conference on track and on time.

Over the years, as I say, my clients have known that there should be more 'interaction' in these affairs. But setting up an 'interactive forum' is not the same as having a real conversation. Setting up an 'interactive forum' at a conference like this is exactly the same as me taking my wife Keri to dinner and me allowing her to involve herself in our dialogue whenever I turn the salt and pepper shakers in her direction. You wouldn't tolerate my behavior in that context, but apparently it's fine in most large group gatherings.

And then we created Town Halls as some sort of giant step forward.

Modern Town Halls are a softening of the edges of large scale gatherings, but the essential shape remains. Someone who is apparently more important than us is at the front of the room and our job is to listen and - at the prescribed time - to ask questions. The person on stage might now be sitting on a high stool or in a director's chair - rather than behind the old, formal table - and they might now be roving the stage with a lavalier microphone and in shirt sleeves. But the essential dynamic remains. There is someone out in front of the gathering, and we are in the behind.

The point here is that the shape, the design, of any meeting confers identity, and therefore behavior.

Much as we have been trained since childhood to sit in rows looking to the front - whether in church or at school - we are hardly bringing our whole selves to an event like that. At many events like this - like Homer Simpson sitting in church, or your being asked to sit through your young child's first band concert - perhaps our best hope is to get out unscathed.

But what if there is more at stake than that? What if we are asked to attend a Town Hall to see what a candidate is really made of?

The Town Hall seems to promise interactivity. So let's get ready for that.

What if we anticipated our attendance, and planned a question we truly wanted to ask that candidate? Not to catch them out, or put them on the spot - but because we have a genuine need to hear their response.

And so we attend the Town Hall and find, for all its apparent informality, that the chances of actually asking our own question is scarce - because there are many others like us with their questions to ask.

And so we wait for the microphone to make its way in our direction. Our tension rises. Much as we are committed to our question, we become very aware that, if we do get to speak, our voice will be magnified - and transmitted to who knows where in whatever media - and what will that feel like?

We are not used to the focus being wholly on us, especially in large gatherings, and if only for a few brief seconds. So we are faced with reading our prepared question from a card - which we know will sound fake and forced - or we'll wing it, with all the risk of sounding stupid that seems to entail if we mumble our words.

Magnify our own, individual trepidation by that of the 100, 200, 300 citizens also in attendance, and now we realize why the room is cooking with anxiety.

And what if we - or someone next to us - gets to ask their question, and the person on stage doesn't give the answer we were expecting? Too late! Now the microphone has been whisked away, and the event MC has taken the conversation into a different direction. We are left feeling unfulfilled. And then angry. And so some people shout at the MC to get the microphone back...and so on.

And now we can see how inevitable it will be that the local TV news station will tomorrow have gleeful coverage of how last night's Town Hall got completely out of hand.

The reporting will be that some 'difficult personalities' caused the upset. But in fact it was inevitable. The outcome was inadvertently forged into the meeting design.

The shape of any meeting confers identity, and therefore behavior.

Public gatherings of citizens, in our current stage of societal development, are examples of conditional communication. The condition is that the leaders get to say their piece, and we get to behave, with reverence and respect, to that speaking.

Our leaders say they need engaged citizens, but that is not going to happen with the forms of meeting we have now. Human engagement happens on an entirely different level than 'sitting listening.'

What would Unconditional Communication look like at the collective level?

Thankfully, one solution is already available. But it requires that those who have spent most of their careers at the front of the room, and still have their hand on the metaphorical salt & pepper shakers to control any interaction, are prepared to give up some of the control they think they are in.

And not give up control so that they are brought down by the crowd, but so that all our collective interactions can co-create something bigger than even the most inspirational leader ever thought possible on their own.

Opening the Space: beyond the Town Hall.

Imagine.

There are 87 members of a community gathered in a large room. They are sitting in three concentric circles of chairs, all facing an empty space in the center. On the floor, in that empty space, there are some paper and pens. On one wall behind the chairs, there is The Big Question - the main theme, challenge or problem this group has gathered to explore. The Big Question begins with the words 'How do we...?' because the Big Question is for all of us, not some of us. On another wall, there is an as yet empty grid labelled The Marketplace. This will become the agenda of the meeting, and will be entirely created by individuals stepping into the circle and writing their ideas, in response to the Big Question, on the papers and sticking them on the Marketplace grid. This is how the big group later will split down into smaller groups to hold the conversations that most matter to them.

This is the start of another Open Space[10] event.

I facilitated an Open Space meeting for my school district recently and witnessed again how much people love it (and not one of them had even heard of the process before). I saw how it so gently and quickly makes people feel that they are heard

---

10. Harrison Owen is the genius who 'accidentally invented' Open Space in the 1980s.

and that their voice matters and (and here's the real point) gets them into *action* on what matters to them. They shift from being worriers about change into being creators of the change.

Now let's jump to the end. One of the things we do at the finale of any Open Space is what is called The Closing Circle - which is simply an opportunity for participants to reflect on their experience. Open Space facilitators know that this way of gathering is different and new for most people, so we give them a chance to talk about it and how it was for them.

One of the things I have consistently heard in The Closing Circle over the years is 'I wish we could do this more often.' They recognize that something significantly different has happened here, compared to what they have been part of in a large group before, and compared with the regular meetings they are used to.

Another thing I have consistently heard in The Closing Circle over the years is 'I had no idea how close we are to each others' perspective.' They get to say this because they have experienced moving from being separate from each other - and believing the stories they've told each other, prior to the event, about how different they are. Here they've been given a space to explore the similarities and concerns they share with others more than their differences.

And one of the things I have consistently seen in The Closing Circle over the years is that 90% of the participants are smiling. It's a smile that reminds me of people at the end of their yoga practice. A serene smile of contentment. Bliss. In yoga, the whole flow is designed to deliver you into the place of the most sacred: the ground of being and presence. The individual returns 'home' to the place where everything began: the void beyond time and space. I think an Open Space does a similar thing in the collective: it takes us to a place where - beneath apparent differences of personality and position - we find that we are all already connected. And that feels good.

Why am I so passionate about Open Space?

Because it works. It is effective in terms of outputs. Problems get solved. Strategies get created. Visions get acted upon. This is not an exercise in Kumbaya[11]. This approach makes substantial things happen.

Let me tell you a little more about why it works in this way. I am going to share this, not because I am trying to sell Open Space to you, but because I have come to realize that the things that make Open Space work in the collective are also profound principles for how any one of us could live our life in an unconditional way.

Open Space has One Law and Four Principles.

The One Law is the Law of Two Feet.

It is sometimes called The Law of Mobility because even if we are in a wheelchair, or hopping on one leg with crutches because of a recent injury, we all have the ability to move our body from here to there. And where we show up in Open Space is going to have a bearing on the outcomes. How we show up

---

11. This is the verbal pushback most leaders new to Open Space use to mask their anxiety about not having all the focus being on them.

when we get there is the purview of the Four Principles, which we'll get to in a minute, and that matters a lot. One thing that doesn't matter is our job title or status. Significantly, in OS, *who* we are - the Big Cheese, the Big Kahuna, the Big Pooh Bah of this group - is of almost no relevance at all.

This is the only Law in Open Space because it is so foundational. The Law of Two Feet or Mobility insists that you are free, and it encourages you to use your freedom to choose which conversations to be part of over the course of the Open Space event. This is offered as a practical tool rather than a philosophical idea. The way OS events are set up, you simply can't be at more than one meeting at the same time (compare that with a traditional conference where you never leave your seat, and all the speakers and panels come and go in front of you), so you have to choose where to go. And you get to choose. There is some simple guidance around this: choose to move to where you feel you can add the most value. That might be based on your personal or professional expertise in relation to the theme being discussed. Or it might be based on your curiosity around it, and willingness to learn. Or simply because you want to go and just listen. All of that, in Open Space, is called being a good citizen.

The Law of Two Feet reminds us that we are all free, even within the responsibilities we have chosen to be part of. We can get married, and choose to be freely married every day. It's only a prison when we say so. We are free to drive our car as far as we want or can afford to buy the gas for, but not free to break the socially agreed speed limits.

The Law of Two Feet is also powerful since it values our contribution. It welcomes our input, whether that looks like our technical brilliance in an area of concern, or simply being present as a good listener to someone else's ideas. All of that is welcome, and valued.

In this way, The Law of Two Feet confers an identity on us as unique and valuable, even when our rational mind is telling us we can only be a faceless unit when we are part of a 200+ strong group of strangers.

And it says, use that identity of value-adding person. Don't take it for granted. Don't leave your value to whither undetected and unheard (unless you choose to use your freedom that way).

Go where it can be put to use. Go where it can serve others, or to the highest purpose available at the time. Don't sit in your chair talking to yourself about why something sounds like a brilliant idea, or one that will never work. Move toward the idea and find out. Move toward the idea and move the idea up the spiral.

In your whole life, whether you take it up or try to ignore it, you will be faced with the Law of Two Feet or Mobility. You are free. Use that freedom seriously, because it is of value, and is creative.

So that is the One Law. Now we come to the Four Principles, which offer us some ideas about how to be with each other.

The First Principle of Open Space is 'Whoever Comes is the Right People.'

In Open Space, this principle is there to remind us that we are not engaged in a popularity contest. The ideas that get taken forward into the action planning stages of an OS event are those that have had the biggest resonance with the group after all the conversations have been reflected on. How many attended each session is simply not part of the decision-making process (attendee names are taken of each session, but only so that they can be invited to continue to participate in the idea after the event). I have seen ideas generated in Open Space events which go on to have major pragmatic impacts on the success of the corporation holding the event, that had only a handful of people discussing the original idea. Open Space is not a poll.

So 'Whoever comes is the right people' means that if you have 50 people at your conversation or 5, value them the same. Because these people are special. They have chosen to be with you at your session when they could equally have used their Two Feet to be elsewhere. They are, by virtue of their presence in the room with you, apparently part of some shared purpose. You invited; they came. How precious is that?

In our lives outside Open Space, we could hold this principle by concerning ourselves with the people who did come to our church service, team meeting or dinner table, rather than being anxious about those who didn't come (and even worse, worrying why they didn't choose to be here). It's a principle that asks us to be appreciative of the potential of what is right now in front of us.

The Second Principle is 'Whenever it Starts is the Right Time.'

The Second Principle reminds that what we are here to generate, whether it be creativity, motivation, insight or commitment, do not work by the clock. They emerge organically. They are formless, are from Spirit, and will be made form at the right time, and almost never because we demand them.

How many of us have had the experience of a conversation, or meeting, that appeared to be going nowhere, and then suddenly 'took off?' Someone says something and then, bang, we are all moving and engaged in 'the real conversation.' The Second Principle encourages us to be patient and willing for that to happen, whenever it does. Because that will be the right time. Pay attention!

The Third Principle is 'When it's Over, it's Over.'

And how many of us stayed too long in relationships not wanting to assert that Principle? There's always an argument for giving things 'just a bit more time' - but there is also power in being able to declare 'I'm done.'

The Third Principle is from the same realm as the Second: it's about how we use our time to the greatest impact, as opposed to simply using time up.

We could all be a lot more effective if we paid more attention to the formless aspects of any meeting than making the form itself the primary thing. When we gather together, the formless is what's trying to come through - the creativity, the connections, the networking, the information shared prior to a decision, the curiosity and the problem-solving. All those are intangible skills and qualities that we should honor and accommodate.

The form of any meeting can be the physical or virtual location. It is its design or shape. And the form of any traditional meeting too often, to its detriment, is 'what the clock is telling us.'

We book an hour of our precious calendar for the weekly meeting about X. My God, how we will fill that hour full of stuff to discuss. Because we don't want to admit we are ever wasting any time, so we pack our meetings about X with so much content, so many presentations, so many words. We want that hour to sweat with content. No pain, no gain. And then we know that we are going to run over, which means that half the participants have started 'keeping an eye on the clock' from about 40 minutes past the hour, wondering how best to extricate themselves from the meeting on time; and then almost all of us still in the room after the hour is done are feeling pissed off about our lack of efficiency, or guilty because now we are late for our next appointment.

The Third Principle says: what if you could keep the other possibility in mind? That you might come to achieve X, and achieve X; and then you can call the meeting done and complete. We don't have to stay here for a whole hour just because we told ourselves it would probably take that long.

When it's over, it's over. When we are done, we declare we are done. And so too for the individual: if I am done with this meeting, if I have contributed what I can, if I don't need to stay just to make someone else confident or affirmed (in which case, I may stay), then why don't I use my two feet to go somewhere else where I can add some value?

It's over for me here, and I am called elsewhere, to add value there.

The Fourth Principle is 'Whatever Happens is the Only Thing that Could Have.'

There is only now.

There is only this present.

You will never have the opportunity to have this conversation ever again. Even if you were able to make these participants turn up next week to have the same meeting about the same topic, it wouldn't be the same conversation, because we are all different by the space of that one week. Can you get the same other 7 people in the same room with you next week? Certainly. Will they have the same conversation? No.

The conversation you are about to have will never happen again, and therefore, when it is done, it is the only thing that could have happened.

So it's fine. If you're only curious about the conversation, then be there and listen. Be a curious presence. Relax and chill into it.

But if you really, really, care, then show up. Pay attention. Challenge the status quo. Speak your truth. Call out BS. So tomorrow you can say, well, it may or may not have happened in the way I was wanting - but I was there, and I communicated unconditionally!

Every conversation you have is a pebble cast into a pond. It may ripple out to the edge and disappear. Or it could be the one that changes a project. A life. A world.

Every hour in every life contains such often-unrecognized potential to affect the world that the great days for which we, in our dissatisfaction, so often yearn are already with us; all great days and thrilling possibilities are combined always in this momentous day.

Reverend Harrison White in
From the Corner of His Eye, Dean Koontz

Finally, there is a bonus principle in Open Space:

Be Prepared to Be Surprised

We have been taught that great leaders have strong positions and points of view. We've been taught to value strength, consistency and predictability.

What has trickled down from that is that we live now in a world fragmented by positions. Inevitably, that most often sounds like 'I'm right, you're wrong.'

So too, we live now in a world of diminishing curiosity. We are losing the capacity to walk a mile in another person's moccasins. We seem less and less able to understand why someone else feels so strongly about a perspective that does not concur with our own. We'd prefer to reinforce why they are wrong and different and separate from us.

In Open Space, we are encouraged to interact in the spirit of curiosity and empathy. It sounds very aspirational. But there is also something in the way that the One Law and the Four Principles operate that make this aspiration more likely to happen. I can't explain it for you. I ask you to try it.

In Open Space, people get surprised: 'I had no idea how close we are to each others' perspective.'

So, to summarize. Open Space works well because it:

- Recognizes the worth of every individual
- Invites the contribution of every participant
- Says you can and will shape the agenda and its outcomes
- Gives prominence to the formless aspects of human engagement - trust and connection - rather than its traditional inputs of content and information
- Says you will choose, and your choice is important and it matters
- Values newness and fresh conversations, rather than re-hashes of old ones
- Invites you to lead and participate however you choose after the event.

Finally, Open Space is an expression of love, as in *lief*. It allows us to be who we are, to share what matters to us, and to do as much or as little as we choose. We get invited, and we get to be free to participate how we choose.

In the face of that invitation to freedom, I have seen consistently that participants in Open Space rise up to that possibility rather than fall from it. I have seen Fifth-graders behave as adults in Open Space, because that's how it treats them.

In other words, Open Space does, at scale, what I believe we most value and appreciate at the interpersonal level with Unconditional Communication.

Unconditional Communication: Micro and Macro

Unconditional Communication, as we have explored in this book, invites us to:

- Recognize the worth and contribution of every individual you communicate with
- Encourages your audience to help shape your idea or agenda and its outcomes
- Gives prominence to the formless aspects of human engagement - trust and connection - rather than its traditional inputs of content and information
- Values 'our way we can create together' over 'my way that I can I persuade you of'
- Invites your audience to lead and participate however they choose after the conversation.

Finally, Unconditional Communication, like Open Space, is an expression of love. It allows your audience to be themselves, without any demand that they be different. Unless they choose to be.

Unconditional Communication, like Open Space, embodies freedom.

So, here we have it: a way of having Unconditional Communication at the micro and the macro levels...and it's all the same thing...natural, focused on co-creating the future, human.

I want to return, one last time, to the end of any Open Space gathering.

Why is most everyone smiling?

Why has the anxiety and tension they felt when they first walked in the room completely dissipated?

What happened between them being freaked out, at the start, by seeing a room set with a circle rather than a row of chairs, to what they are thinking now?

Why do they feel so much better?

Because they've spent the last few hours not as separate identities, crammed into that anxious container they call their life, but as part of a collective, part of a Whole that made them feel heard and supported and safe and at home *and strong*.

It is gathering as a spiritual practice. Who'd have thought that was possible?

A CONTRAST BETWEEN TWO WAYS OF GATHERING

Open Space is opposite to our experience of traditional large group gatherings. Traditional ones are also are driven by One Law and Four Principles, strangely enough. These are:

The Law of Parenting
People wiser than you have worked out why this gathering is important, and what success looks like for them. There is nothing you need to be concerned about, other than paying attention to the rules of engagement.

Principle One
We will tell you who the right people are; they are on the seating list for your table, or they have a sticker of the same color on their name badge as you. This is what makes them the right people. We arranged this. Even if we tried to mix things up in terms of diversity, that was planned in advance by us.

As a bonus, because you have behaved well in the past, we will tell you exactly what conversations to have, and when to be back here to report to us all how insightful those conversations have been.

or

The right people are the most senior, qualified people and they were too busy to be here today, so this meeting is going to be a waste of time.

Principle Two
It starts when we say so; how obvious does this need to be for you?

Principle Three
It's over when the boss needs to leave; you can follow later.

or

We want to 'honor your time' by closing exactly at the predetermined endpoint, so, even though we haven't created anything of value yet, we are going to close down this meeting so we can all go off and waste our time elsewhere in a similar fashion.

Principle Four
What happens is what we say will happen; any deviation from that good news is not required. We have seen the future and it will work for us.

By the way, being prepared to be surprised is seditious nonsense, and will be treated accordingly.

These, then, are the rules of collective Traditional Conditional Communication.

I am teasing here. A little. I hope I have not been part of a gathering where the organizers were coming from these extremely explicit standpoints of control and power. Yet the road to hell is paved with good intentions, and no design ever emerged out of nothing. Design always stands upon a grounding of principles and assumptions. If you didn't know of Open Space, and simply attended one, eventually you would infer something like its One Law and Four Principles. Similarly, if you reflect on the last few conferences and traditional large group meetings you've attended, you'd realize that they are based on suppositions and rules not too far from those I've just described.

As soon as you begin to lay out a room so that everyone can see the screen at the front of it, you have begun to strangle the capacity of the Creators about to gather there.

If Town Halls, organized debates - and any large scale gathering based on a triangle facing the front of the room - were giving us what we were really looking for, if they were tapping into the best of us all, if they were equipping us to deal with the wicked, complex problems of our societies, then I'd be happy to stay silent. But that is not the case. Eventually we have to stop looking to the front of the room for our salvation, and turn to each other.

If we allow our leaders to not challenge their own fear that without control and micromanagement there will be chaos, then we are insulting the people they invite. Insisting that the best possible outcome for an event is that those leaders sound strong, persuasive and 'leader-like', always leaves the talents of the many, and the seeds of possibility, ungerminated.

The times are calling for a better, bigger way to organize, so we can move on the Upward Spiral, together.

NOT THE END

The 'War of the Worlds' Effect

I'll leave you with one final thought. It's not a prescription to act upon, or even a conclusion as such. Instead, it's something that will hopefully ground your understanding of unconditional communication, and more specifically, demonstrate how innate it is to all of us, and how simple it ought to be to exercise it.

It's that communication is human.

It is as human as breathing air or drinking water.

It is natural.

It is instinctive.

It is essential to our survival.

And, perhaps most importantly, it makes us feel good.

Unconditional Communication

Our brains enjoy communicating and collaborating with others. It may frustrate us and confound us when it goes wrong, but it is undeniably pleasurable when it goes right. It feels good to come to an agreement. It feels good to learn new things. And it feels good to connect with others, to feel as they feel, and to see the world from their perspective.

Nowhere is this clearer than in the art of storytelling. Over the long, sprawling, history of mankind – from caves to castles, to cities and suburbs – storytelling has always been, and will always be, part of humanity's cultural DNA.

We still have records of The Epic of Gilgamesh, and the Enûma Eliš, works of literature and spiritualism that date back to 2000 years before Christ.

Before we even wrote anything down, we maintained vibrant oral storytelling traditions in civilizations across the globe – enshrining our histories, our values, and our cultures in tales and poems that, even today, inform our humanity and our sense of purpose.

The oldest cave paintings we've discovered were painted over 40,000 years ago.

And those are just what we've discovered.

In other words, storytelling, like love, is universal. We come by it naturally and gravitate towards it instinctively. We don't have to teach children to take lessons from stories – in much the same way that we don't have to teach children to love. We just read them the story and their humanity does the rest, because also like love, we experience storytelling biologically, as well as intellectually and emotionally.

When we engage with a story, whether written, spoken, painted, or played, we experience real, physiological reactions. When something is distressing, our brain releases cortisol which captures our attention and keeps us focused. When something is compelling or interesting, our brain releases dopamine, which rewards us with pleasure and excitement. And when someone, or something, stirs our sympathy, our brain releases oxytocin to help us relate and identify with our protagonist.

It happens whether we like it or not. Have you ever caught yourself watching a movie you assumed you would hate, only to find yourself enthralled by it? Have you ever kept watching one, even though Ratty says that you have something better to do?

My Mum has.

It is October 30, 2019. I'm in the living room with Mum at our home in Loveland, Colorado.

For the last 10 of her 87 years, she's lived inside the story that she was too old or frail to travel to visit us in Colorado. Then something, suddenly, gave way, and I guess she realized that she didn't like her role in that story, nor how the story was likely going to end. So she got herself a new story, and got on the plane from her home in Churwell, UK.

Three weeks into her stay with us, we surprise her with a trip to San Francisco. We wanted her to know that, having done an international, long haul flight, she could enjoy a shorter one too.

It's been a visit of surprises, for all of us. She'd never eaten Chinese Food before. And she'd never been up close to a sky-scraper. Nor had she ever seen streets like the streets of San Francisco. But she has now.

So it's now Wednesday evening around 8pm, and we are just back in Loveland from San Francisco, and she's sitting down to enjoy a cup of tea before bed. As always, there's not much on TV, so I flick through the channels and find that Spielberg's version of *The War of the Worlds* is on.

And my Mum starts watching *The War of the Worlds*. She's looking tired. It's been a long day for her, a day of hotels and Ubers and airports and flights and then a long drive home, in the dark, from DIA on some snowy and icy roads.

I wait for her to finish her cup of tea, and expect her at any moment to announce, as she usually does at around this time, "Well, I'd better get ready for bed!"

But instead she watches. And watches.

Clearly, she has no common experience with these protagonists threatened by an invasion of deadly aliens. But she does know human beings, and, no doubt against her internal dialogue telling her 'I ought to go to bed,' she finds herself caring for these characters and their futures.

She cares little for science fiction as a format, but she does know danger, and threat, and the desire to fight, and the drive to live at all costs.

She doesn't understand CGI, but she does understand heroism, and innocence lost. And she knows what it means to be a parent and to protect your children.

About 50 minutes in, I remind her that we do have the technology to pause the movie and finish watching it tomorrow. But she says, 'No. I want to see how it ends.'

And she does.

This is how storytelling works. Even as Ratty can chatter away in us about how bad the writing sometimes is, and how wooden some of the actors are, and how unrealistic and unlikely some of the plot is, our innate tendency towards storytelling, towards collaboration, towards oneness and understanding, will drown Ratty out with such force that we can become fully immersed in a co-created reality.

The point I'm making is not that *The War of the Worlds* is a particularly fantastic movie. It's not. 75% Rotten Tomatoes. 73% Metacritic. Yes, that's about right. The point I'm making is that storytelling, like unconditional communication, is capable of overcoming the barriers we put up to separate ourselves. And beyond overcoming that separation, capable of joining us together under one cohesive understanding.

Ratty is exceptionally good at building these barriers, at reinforcing these anxieties, and at providing justifications for doing so. But nature has provided humans with a natural and innate ability to circumvent them – to connect, regardless of context or concrete concern.

We have always had, and will always have, the means to create these connections, in much the same way that Alan and I, as we scrapped our set, were confident that we would always have the means to create Gulliver's world for our audience. It is innate within us – inseparable from what makes us human – and essential to the continuation of civilization. It is what ties us together, even when all we want to see is difference and distance.

Of course, life is more complicated than *The War of the Worlds*. We have to have conversations that are more complex than Wednesday night entertainment.

Unlike the story that is *The War of the Worlds*, life is messy and awkward and often ugly, and in this way, unconditional communication, at its core, is really more like poetry than a movie or a novel. Not like a Robert Frost poem, where everything is clean and clear, but more like a T.S. Eliot poem.

If you came this way,
Taking any route, starting from anywhere,
At any time or at any season,
It would always be the same: you would have to put off
Sense and notion. You are not here to verify,
Instruct yourself, or inform curiosity
Or carry report. You are here to kneel
Where prayer has been valid. And prayer is more
Than an order of words, the conscious occupation
Of the praying mind, or the sound of the voice praying.
And what the dead had no speech for, when living,
They can tell you, being dead: the communication
Of the dead is tongued with fire beyond the language of the living.

From *Little Gidding*, TS Eliot

Eliot is rightfully regarded as one of the greatest linguists in English literature. Few poets have equaled his mastery of the complexities and fallacies of language, and fewer still have employed that mastery as deftly as he did. In terms of being a creator through our words, he was arguably one of the best.

That's not to say that he communicated clearly, or even beautifully (though I personally find his poems beautiful). If we were to grade famous communicators according to their charisma and persuasiveness, Hitler would certainly be far higher on our list.

Eliot's poems are often esoteric, obscure, and ugly. They challenge us in ways that a speech, or an essay, or an article, or *The War of the Worlds*, would never challenge us; they invite us to look past an easy summation, to grapple and engage with the messiness that most communication hides.

In other words, nobody has ever finished a T.S. Eliot poem and thought to themselves, "he's right about _____."

Poetry, like unconditional communication does not require a final answer. It doesn't depend on your understanding it, or agreeing with it, or hating it. It's simply an invitation to a conversation between reader and author. And from that conversation, without fail, blossoms new and exciting insights, perspectives, and opportunities, which would never have lived without that intrinsic open-endedness.

There is no right answer that unconditional communication will produce for us – no immediate understanding – no digestible soundbite to comfort us – no neatly packaged solution to the problems we face. Instead, unconditional communication offers us a chance to connect, uninhibited by expectation, apprehension, or anxiety.

It offers us a new path forward; an ever growing upward spiral, actualized by presence, supported by togetherness, and propelled by co-created outcomes.

My eldest son, Oliver, has had two major journeys in his life already. The first was when he spent 3 months in Europe. As I write this, he is six months into a two year stay in Japan. For the next two years, his home is a small city, Esashi, population 8000, give or take, in Hokkaido. He has a government-sponsored job with the local school district, tasked with raising the capacity for English-speaking among teachers, students, and the wider community. He'll learn invaluable lessons that come with having any job, working out the flow between personal expression and the expectations of his employers. But his primary reason for being there, he is clear, is to become fluent in Japanese, as this is critical for his future career as an academic. He'd completed two years of learning Japanese at the University of Denver, but there is a difference between classroom learning and an immersion in the culture.

The other day we were speaking on Line (the Japanese text/voice app), and I asked him how his Japanese was coming along.

He told me the story of having a conversation recently with someone in the community about something they needed to make a decision together on, I can't recall the details. But I do remember Ollie explaining the difference between what's going on regularly for him now, compared with his travels through Europe in his 'gap year' (strange term, 'gap,' for a year that had so much richness in it!).

And here is the difference he shared with me: that when his Japanese is not good enough to produce an easy understanding in his audience, he can't expect there'll be a fallback like when he was in Germany, for example. That when his German was not good enough, his German counterparts would always be able to slip into near-perfect English and rescue the conversation. Where he is in Japan, there is no such fallback available. His Japanese halts, and his Japanese counterparts have almost zero English.

And so what occurs then, he tells me, is patience, and persistence, and a desire to somehow connect, despite the lack of technically correct and shared language. They make a subtle agreement that they will find a way forward, together. That connection will matter more than the reasons to have a problem.

In other words, there is unconditional communication, driven by empathy and creativity, and care.

As we discussed at the beginning of this book, it is unlikely that the world around us, our politicians, our journalists, or our corporations will make this transition with us, or even understand it. After all, there is far too much at stake in being a powerful conditional communicator. We have rewarded persuasion and its champions whenever and wherever they have arisen, and the odds are, society at large will continue to do so.

But that doesn't mean that you and I need to blindly flog that dead horse any longer. We can shape the trajectory of our lives and indeed the very nature of human communication by taking the reins of discourse and gripping them with the intentionality, conviction, and love of which we are all capable.

It sounds difficult. And it is.

But that doesn't make it not worth doing; in fact it makes it all the more noble, all the more invigorating, and indeed all the more human. It's not about being perfect, it's not about always saying the right thing, and it's not about winning – it's about taking your place as a creator in this world and assuming all the privileges, duties, and responsibilities that come with it. It's about giving yourself to others, and embracing togetherness as a state of being, rather than as a strategy or tactic to pursue your own interests.

It's about vulnerability and honesty and humility and strength.

Our hero's journey—which begins with the revelation that our society and its institutions are not co-created and probably never will be—ends a little differently than that of the heroes to whom we might compare ourselves. We are not destroying the death star or the one ring or the dragon—we are not saving the world once and for all—we are instead discovering something far more complex: that life has meaning, and purpose, and value, and that we are responsible for creating it. Whether we want to or not.

When we take that first step, committing to intentionality in all we say and do, we begin to actively shape our journey, and as we begin to shape our own, we will also shape the journeys of those around us. We will falter and struggle, but as long as we continue to pursue that intentionality, that awareness, and that sense of purpose, together, we will continue along the upward spiral of human progress.

Our hero's journey has no finite conclusion, no final return on which we can sign our signature and say, "all done." For our journey is part and parcel of the ever forming upward spiral of our lives and the lives of humans everywhere. Our journey is unending, unpredictable, and unlimited.

I leave you with this one message, which, if you forget everything else in this book, I sincerely hope you always remember.

Life, as TS Eliot intimated at the end of *Little Gidding*, has meaning, and purpose, and is precious.

And, at last, there is something beyond curiosity and searching and even praying ...it is called

Reverence

Awe

and

Gratitude.

About the Author

My consulting firm is a channel for Presence, Connection and Co-created Outcomes.

David Firth is a channel for Love.

www.davidfirth.com

Other Books by David Firth

How to Make Work Fun!

The Corporate Fool

From 'Making a Living' to Creating a Life

Change your World, One Word at a Time

Rise

Coming soon:

How to Communicate Good